101 Spanish Proverbs

Understanding Spanish Language and Culture Through Common Sayings

101

Spanish
Proverbs

Eduardo Aparicio • Illustrated by Luc Nisset

New York   Chicago   San Francisco   Lisbon   London   Madrid   Mexico City
Milan   New Delhi   San Juan   Seoul   Singapore   Sydney   Toronto

1 2 3 4 5 6 7 8 9 10 11 12 13 14 15 16 17 18 19 20 21   FGR/FGR   0 9

ISBN 978-0-07-161558-7 (book and MP3 disk set)
MHID   0-07-161558-X (book and MP3 disk set)

ISBN 978-0-07-161559-4 (book for set)
MHID   0-07-161559-8 (book for set)

Library of Congress Control Number: 2008935416

MP3 Files

The disk contains MP3 audio recordings that accompany the book.

To download: Double-click on MY COMPUTER, find and open your CD-ROM disk drive and double-click on the 101 Spanish Proverbs icon.

The MP3 files can be played on your computer and loaded onto your MP3 player. For optimum use on the iPod:

1. Open iTunes on your computer.
2. Drag folder "Copy to iTunes Music Library" into the Music Library in the iTunes menu.
3. Sync your iPod with iTunes and eject iPod.
4. Locate recordings on your iPod by following this path:
    Main menu: Music
    Music menu: Artists
    Artist menu: Spanish: 101 Proverbs

Call 1-800-722-4726 if the MP3 disk is missing from this book.
For technical support go to
http://www.mhprofessional.com/support/technical/contact.php

This book is printed on acid-free paper.

Contents

Las paredes oyen □ No hay pan sin corteza □ En boca cerrada no entran moscas □ A caballo regalado no se le mira el colmillo □ Aunque la mona se vista de seda, mona se queda □ Antes de hacer nada, consúltalo con la almohada □ El que se fue a Sevilla, perdió la silla □ Cada quien es el arquitecto de su propio destino □ Un lugar para cada cosa y cada cosa en su lugar □ No hay peor sordo que el que no quiere oír □ Agua que no has de beber, déjala correr □ El que dice lo que quiere, oye lo que no quiere □ Haz lo que yo digo y no lo que yo hago □ Oficio quita vicio □ A lo hecho, pecho □ Más vale ser cabeza de ratón que cola de león

Más sabe el diablo por viejo que por diablo □ De tal palo, tal astilla □ Cuando el diablo no tiene qué hacer, con el rabo mata moscas □ Niño que no llora no mama □ Nunca es tarde para aprender □ Lo que se aprende en la cuna, hasta la sepultura acompaña □ Los niños y los locos dicen las verdades □ El diente miente, la cana engaña, pero la arruga no ofrece duda □ El que no oye consejo no llega a viejo □ Árbol que nace torcido jamás su tronco endereza

Hombre prevenido vale por dos □ Piensa el ladrón que todos son de su condición □ El hábito no hace al monje □ El que ríe último ríe mejor □ Quien nada sabe, de nada duda □ Quien estudia y no aprende, si no es asno lo parece □ De noche todos los gatos son pardos □ Mucho hablar y poco decir juntos suelen ir □ Unos dicen lo que saben y otros saben lo que dicen □ Ojos que no ven, corazón que no siente □ Al César lo que es del César y a Dios lo que es de Dios □ Aprendiz de todo y maestro de nada □ Vale más una imagen que mil palabras □ Vale más una verdad amarga que muchas mentiras dulces □ El saber no ocupa lugar □ No hay tonto, por tonto que sea, que tonto se crea

Foreword

Proverbs, by stating basic principles of traditional wisdom and conduct, are an integral part of daily speech in modern languages.

Each language has its own proverbs. In some cases, the phrasing of a Spanish proverb is unique and represents a particular view of life from the vantage point of Hispanic culture. In other cases, a Spanish proverb can have an almost identical English-language equivalent. Very often the precepts of one culture are the precepts of another, for they are an outgrowth of common experiences.

Proverbs are relatively easy for nonnative speakers to learn and use. Once the concept of the proverb is understood, students can often relate it to similar concepts, in their own languages.

101 Spanish Proverbs is designed to help students of Spanish understand and use proverbs that relate to everyday situations. For this reason, the proverbs in this book are grouped in seven thematic sections. This logical positioning of the proverbs facilitates student understanding and acquisition of proverbs for use in particular contexts.

The proverbs included in **101 Spanish Proverbs** are among those that are most familiar to and most frequently used by native speakers of Spanish. Each proverb is presented in its most common form, together with a literal translation in parenthesis and an equivalent English-language proverb below it. The wording and definitions selected for this book are intended to help students achieve a basic understanding of each proverb.

A cartoon and a short dialogue are also provided to help illustrate the meaning and usage of each proverb. The dialogues serve two purposes: to give an understanding of the proverb in a normal, everyday setting, and to enhance the student's awareness of natural speech in Spanish. The illustrations add an element of humor while helping to convey the meaning of each proverb.

Translations of the dialogues have been provided at the back of the book as a further aid to understanding. An index is also included to facilitate recall and location of the proverbs.

101 Spanish Proverbs is an excellent tool for teaching an aspect of Spanish that is such an integral part of the language. This book is intended for anyone who has an interest in learning more about the Spanish language and Hispanic culture. Whether you are currently studying Spanish, are planning a trip to a Spanish-speaking country, or simply want a glimpse of how Hispanic culture views the world, you will find yourself referring to this collection of colorful Spanish proverbs. Both native and nonnative speakers of Spanish will benefit from and enjoy the wealth of linguistic and cultural information to be found in this selection of **101 Spanish Proverbs.**

Section One
Buenos consejos
Good Advice

1 Las paredes oyen

(the walls hear)
walls have ears

—Manuel, tengo un secreto que contarte.

—¿De qué se trata, Isabel?

—Es algo que me dijeron de ti.

—Dímelo ahora mismo.

—No, ahora mismo no, aquí en la oficina no es buen lugar. Tú sabes que **las paredes oyen**. Y en esta oficina, la gente es muy chismosa. Mejor nos vemos en el parque cuando salgamos del trabajo.

—Sí. Aquí en la oficina, **alguien nos puede oír sin darnos cuenta.**

—Bueno, te espero en el parque y te lo cuento todo.

2 No hay pan sin corteza

(there is no bread without crust)
cold hands, warm heart

—Tu padre parece un hombre exigente y rígido.

—Pues no. Es todo lo contrario. Mi padre es un hombre cariñoso, comprensivo y bueno. Él da esa impresión porque ha tenido muchas dificultades en la vida. Tú sólo lo conoces por fuera. Yo lo conozco por dentro.

—Te entiendo. Como dice mi abuela: **No hay pan sin corteza.**

—Efectivamente. **Hay personas que parecen muy duras por fuera pero son muy buenas por dentro.**

4

3 En boca cerrada no entran moscas

(in a closed mouth flies do not enter)
a closed mouth catches no flies

—Mi suegra está enojadísima conmigo, Carmen.

—¿Qué pasó?

—Simplemente le recomendé un programa de dieta muy bueno, pues está muy gorda.

—¿Quién te habrá mandado a decirle eso? Es mejor no decirle nada. Ya sabes que **en boca cerrada no entran moscas.**

—Yo sólo quise darle un buen consejo.

—Pero recuerda que a veces **es mejor callar porque el hablar trae problemas.**

—¡Tienes toda la razón del mundo! Tendré que tener más cuidado con lo que digo.

4 A caballo regalado no se le mira el colmillo

(do not look a gift horse in the eye tooth)
don't look a gift horse in the mouth

—¡Hola, Carlos! ¿Qué tal te va con tu nueva computadora?

—Bueno, no es nada del otro mundo.

—¿No fue el regalo que te hicieron tus padres por tu cumpleaños?

—Sí, pero es una pequeña computadora portátil que sólo me sirve para hacer los trabajos de mis cursos en la universidad y comunicarme por el Internet. Pero la pantalla no es a colores y no tiene ninguno de los juegos computarizados que a mí me gustan.

—¡Pero, Carlos! ¿De qué te quejas? **A caballo regalado no se le mira el colmillo.** Ojalá mis padres me regalaran a mí una computadora como la tuya.

—Sí, tienes razón. **No es justo que me queje de algo que me han regalado.**

5 Aunque la mona se vista de seda, mona se queda

(even though the monkey dresses in silk, she stays a monkey)

you can't make a silk purse out of a sow's ear

[Esperanza y su esposo están en una recepción muy elegante en honor a un diplomático que está de visita.]

—¡Qué elegante se ve Rebeca hoy! —comenta Esperanza—. Nunca la había visto con un vestido tan caro.

—Tendrá un vestido muy caro, pero sus malos modales no han cambiado.

—Se nota su mal gusto en su manera de hablar. Ahora está hablando con la boca llena. Eso prueba que **aunque la mona se vista de seda, mona se queda.**

—Desgraciadamente, **la persona no puede esconder su falta de educación ni sus malos modales aunque se ponga ropa cara.**

6 Antes de hacer nada, consúltalo con la almohada

(before doing anything, consult it with the pillow)
it's better to sleep on it

—Esa inversión es grande, Alina. ¿Has pensado bien en los riesgos que trae consigo?

—Sí —responde Alina, no muy convencida.

—Por la forma en que lo dices, no lo creo. Fíjate, **antes de hacer nada, consúltalo con la almohada.**

—¿Con la almohada?

—Sí. **Espera hasta mañana para tomar una decisión.** Así tendrás más tiempo para pensar sobre el asunto.

—Sí, mejor es esperar un día más antes de firmar los papeles y entregar un cheque. Lo voy a pensar bien.

7 El que se fue a Sevilla, perdió la silla

(he who went to Seville lost his chair)
possession is nine-tenths of the law

[Un joven está en el cine. La película no ha empezado todavía. El joven escoge un asiento y deja una revista en él para reservarlo. Va a buscar un refresco y cuando regresa un señor ha tomado su asiento.]

—Disculpe, señor, pero ese asiento es mío.

—¿Es suyo, joven? ¿Usted lo trajo de su casa?

—No, no lo traje de mi casa, pero yo estaba sentado allí. Me fui a buscar un refresco y dejé una revista en el asiento para guardarlo.

—Lo siento, joven. **El que se fue a Sevilla, perdió la silla.** Su revista está ahora en el asiento de atrás.

—¿Pero, con qué derecho?

—Mire, joven, usted abandonó su lugar. **El que abandona su lugar, cuando regrese, es normal que lo encuentre ocupado.** La culpa es suya, no mía.

8 Cada quien es el arquitecto de su propio destino

(each one is the architect of his own destiny)
every man is the architect of his own fortune

—¿Sabes que este cura nuevo que tenemos en la iglesia tiene ideas muy modernas?

—¿Qué ideas tiene?

—Yo me estaba quejando de la mala suerte que he tenido en mi vida. Nunca he tenido un buen trabajo, mi mujer me dejó por ser borracho, mis hijos no quieren venir a visitarme. Yo pensé que era la culpa del diablo, pero el cura me dijo: **cada quien es el arquitecto de su propio destino.**

—Yo estoy de acuerdo con él. **Cada uno es responsable de su vida y de mejorarla con su propio esfuerzo y trabajo.**

9 Un lugar para cada cosa y cada cosa en su lugar

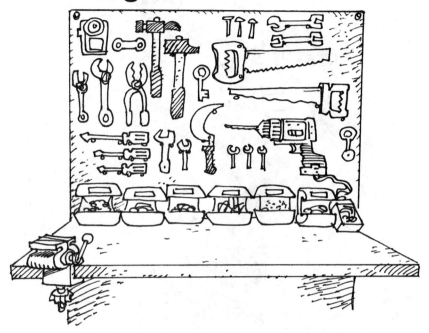

(a place for each thing and each thing in its place)
a place for everything and everything in its place

—No encuentro mi libreta de teléfonos. ¿La has visto? ¿Dónde la habré puesto?

—¿Cómo vas a saber? ¡Mira lo desordenado que tienes tu cuarto!

—Es una libretica de tapa azul. Tienes que haberla visto.

—No he visto nada. Si tuvieras **un lugar para cada cosa y cada cosa en su lugar,** ya la hubieras encontrado.

—Sí, ya sé, mamá, **hay que ser organizado.** Me lo has dicho muchas veces, pero ahora estoy apurado y necesito la libreta.

—Y si sabes que debes ser más organizado, ¿por qué no lo haces? Mira, aquí tienes tu libretica. Estaba en la cocina. Con tanto espacio que tienes al lado del teléfono, y la dejas en la cocina. No sé hasta cuándo vas a ser así.

10 No hay peor sordo que el que no quiere oír

**(there is no worse deaf man than he who does
not want to hear)**

there's none so deaf as those who
will not hear

—Carlos, hace rato que te dije que sacaras la basura.

—¿Estás segura, mamá? Yo no te oí.

—No hay peor...

—Sí, ya sé... **No hay peor sordo que el que no quiere oír**.
Todos los días me dices lo mismo.

—Es que **tú oyes sólo lo que te conviene.** Estoy cansada de
decirte las cosas y que no me hagas caso.

11 Agua que no has de beber, déjala correr

(water that you shall not drink, let it run)
let sleeping dogs lie

—Rafael, ¿has visto el nuevo novio de Rosa?

—Sí, es un hombre mucho mayor que ella.

—La verdad es que no me explico por qué Rosa tiene un novio así. Ella es tan joven, bonita e inteligente. Se merece alguien joven igual que ella.

—¡Ay, Alberto! **Agua que no has de beber, déjala correr.**

—¿Por qué me dices eso?

—Tú tienes tu novia y nunca estuviste interesado en Rosa. Deja que Rosa tome las decisiones de su vida. **No te metas en asuntos que no son tuyos.**

12 El que dice lo que quiere, oye lo que no quiere

(he who says what he wants, hears what he does not want)
a word once spoken is past recalling

—¿Viste la entrevista anoche con Miss Universo por la televisión?

—El periodista era muy malo. Le dijo a Miss Universo que él no entendía por qué ella había ganado el concurso.

—Y Miss Universo le contestó muy bien. Le dijo que era natural que él no entendiera pues su belleza y talento sólo lo pueden apreciar las personas inteligentes.

—Le contestó muy bien. **El que dice lo que quiere, oye lo que no quiere.**

—Miss Universo le demostró que **hay que pensar bien lo que uno va a decir antes de hablar.**

13 Haz lo que yo digo y no lo que yo hago

(do what I say and not what I do)
do as I say, not as I do

—Rigoberto, esta tarde te vi fumando. Como padre, tengo la obligación de darte un consejo. El tabaco hace daño a la salud. Eres muy joven; es mejor que dejes de fumar.

—¿Tú, diciéndome que deje de fumar? De ti mismo lo aprendí. En los 19 años que tengo, siempre te he visto fumar. Lo tuyo es de **haz lo que yo digo y no lo que yo hago.** ¿Verdad?

—Tienes razón, **no está bien querer prohibirle algo a los demás y no a uno mismo.** Pero es que yo ya llevo muchos años fumando y es difícil dejarlo. Ojalá mi padre me hubiera convencido para que dejara de fumar cuando yo tenía tu edad.

14 Oficio quita vicio

(occupation takes away vice)
work helps you stay out of trouble

—¡Hola, Lalo! ¿Cómo estás, hombre? ¿En qué andas?

—Estoy bien, Rodolfo, pero muy ocupado. Conseguí un trabajo.

—¿Trabajo? ¡No lo puedo creer! ¿Y hasta cuándo te va a durar esa enfermedad?

—No es ninguna enfermedad. Me gusta este trabajo y lo quiero conservar. Tú deberías hacer lo mismo, hombre.

—¿Qué me sugieres? ¿Que **oficio quita vicio,** como dice el refrán?

—Claro, Rodolfo. Antes tú y yo siempre andábamos de vagos jugando billar, mirando la tele, desperdiciando el tiempo. **Trabajar es una forma de ocupar el tiempo en algo productivo y de evitar malas costumbres.**

—Te has puesto muy aburrido. Deja de darme consejos.

15 A lo hecho, pecho

(to what's done, chest)
what's done is done

—¡Vamos, corran muchachos! Tenemos que irnos antes de que salgan los dueños de la casa.

—No creo que debamos irnos, Jaime. Tenemos que decirles que fuimos nosotros.

—¿Estás loco, Miguel? Seguro llaman a la policía y a nuestros padres. ¡Yo no quiero meterme en líos!

—No sean cobardes, chicos. **A lo hecho, pecho.**

—Oye, Miguel. Es cierto que **tenemos que hacernos responsables de nuestras acciones y enfrentarnos a las consecuencias.** Pero no nos digas cobardes, que me ofendo. Te acepto malos lanzadores y peores bateadores, eso sí.

—¡Caramba, Luis! ¿Por qué será que se te olvidó decir pésimos jardineros?

16 Más vale ser cabeza de ratón que cola de león

**(better to be the head of a mouse
than the tail of a lion)**
better be the head of a dog than
the tail of a lion

—Mirta, ¿es cierto que dejas tu trabajo y te vas a una compañía pequeña?

—Sí, ya lo decidí. Me voy el mes que viene.

—¿Te parece buena idea? ¿No es mejor trabajar para una compañía grande, con más prestigio y mejores oportunidades?

—Depende cómo lo veas. En la compañía grande nunca voy a tener un puesto importante. Llevo tres años en el mismo lugar. Pero en la compañía pequeña me ofrecieron un puesto de gerente.

—Ya veo, tú pensaste: **más vale ser cabeza de ratón que cola de león.**

—Así mismo, para mí **es mejor ser líder de algo pequeño en lugar de ser la última en algo grande.**

—¡Pues buena suerte en tu nuevo trabajo!

Section Two
Jóvenes y viejos
The Young and Old

17 Más sabe el diablo por viejo que por diablo

(the devil knows more from being old than from being the devil)
the devil knows many things
because he is old

—Fernando, ¿qué piensas de nuestro nuevo entrenador de natación? A mí me parece que está demasiado mayor. Yo prefiero tener un entrenador más joven.

—Yo pensé lo mismo la primera vez que lo vi. Pero me he dado cuenta que tiene mucha experiencia y sabe lo que hace.

—¿Pero no crees que sería mejor tener un entrenador joven?

—No necesariamente: recuerda que **más sabe el diablo por viejo que por diablo.**

—Es cierto. Fue campeón de natación de joven. Hace muchos años que enseña. **La edad es una ventaja porque representa más experiencia.**

—Exactamente. Un entrenador joven no sería tan bueno como él.

18 De tal palo, tal astilla

(from such wood, such splinter)
like father, like son

—Margarita, no sé qué hacer con mi hijo. Los domingos se pasa el día entero mirando los deportes en la televisión. Ya tiene 17 años. Sería mejor que dedicara el tiempo a estudiar o a trabajar.

—Yo creo que él no tiene la culpa. Su padre hace lo mismo. **De tal palo tal astilla.**

—Sí, **mi hijo tiene las mismas malas costumbres que su padre.**

—Lo mejor es que hables con él para que se dé cuenta que está perdiendo mucho tiempo mirando televisión. A su edad hay que aprovechar el tiempo para estudiar o trabajar.

19 Cuando el diablo no tiene qué hacer, con el rabo mata moscas

(when the devil has nothing to do, he kills flies with his tail)

the devil finds work for idle hands to do

[Sonia es profesora en la universidad y acaba de llegar a casa. Allí la esperan su esposo Vicente y sus dos niños.]

—¿Qué tal pasaron la tarde? ¿Los niños hicieron la tarea?

—Tenían muy poca tarea que hacer. Terminaron enseguida y los dejé jugando con tu computadora.

—¿Jugando con mi computadora?

—Y las noticias no son muy buenas. Parece que te borraron varios documentos.

—¿Por qué no les diste más tarea o te pusiste a estudiar con ellos? Tú sabes que **cuando el diablo no tiene qué hacer, con el rabo mata moscas.**

—Tienes razón, no debí haberlos dejado solos con tu computadora. **Los niños, cuando no tienen qué hacer, hacen alguna travesura.**

20 Niño que no llora no mama

(child who does not cry does not nurse)
the squeaky wheel gets the oil

—Ayer me pasó algo muy desagradable en el restaurante. El mesero se demoró mucho en atenderme. Era un restaurante elegante y a mí me daba pena llamarlo en voz alta.

—¿Y dónde estaba el mesero que no te atendía?

—Había otra mesa con una señora con muy malos modales. No le daba pena gritar y alzar los brazos para llamarlo.

—Ya sabes que **niño que no llora no mama.**

—Yo creo que en un restaurante hay que tener buenos modales. A mí me da pena alzar la voz. Pero es cierto que **los que se quejan más reciben mejor atención.**

21 Nunca es tarde para aprender

(it's never too late to learn)
you're never too old to learn

—¿A dónde vas tan elegante, Jaime?

—Voy a la graduación de mi abuelita.

—¿La graduación de tu abuelita? No entiendo.

—Sí, acaba de terminar sus estudios universitarios. Dice que de joven no tenía dinero ni tiempo para estudiar y que **nunca es tarde para aprender.**

—¿Qué fue lo que estudió tu abuelita?

—Estudió historia. Pensó que con todos los años que ha vivido, le sería fácil estudiar historia.

—¡Qué bueno! Eso demuestra que **los estudios no son sólo para los jóvenes, sino para cualquier edad.** Felicítame a tu abuelita.

—¡Gracias, Mirta! Bueno, me voy. Si no, yo sí que voy a llegar tarde.

22 Lo que se aprende en la cuna, hasta la sepultura acompaña

(what is learned in the cradle will accompany you to the grave)
what's learned in the cradle lasts
'til the tomb

—Julito es un muchacho muy bueno.

—Sus abuelos lo criaron muy bien. Es estudioso, respetuoso y trabajador.

—Sí, menos mal que lo criaron sus abuelos. Ya sabemos que su madre y su padre son un poco locos y desordenados.

—Gracias a sus abuelos tiene muy buenas cualidades. Y ahora que se va a estudiar a la universidad, ¿crees que cambiará?

—En lo absoluto, no lo creo. **Lo que se aprende en la cuna, hasta la sepultura acompaña.**

—Tienes razón, **las costumbres que se aprenden de niño permanecen toda la vida.**

23 Los niños y los locos dicen las verdades

(children and the insane tell truths)
out of the mouths of babes

—¿Cómo les fue en el viaje? ¿La pasaron bien?

—Ay, mi amor, qué pena me ha hecho pasar nuestra hija en el aeropuerto.

—¿Laurita? ¿Por qué? ¿Qué hizo?

—Imagínate, que antes de salir, en el salón de espera, todos los asientos estaban ocupados. ¿Y sabes lo que hizo tu hija? Se acercó a uno de los hombres sentados y le dijo: "¿Usted no ve que mi mamá está en estado? ¿Puede hacerme el favor de darle el asiento?"

—¡Ah, ésa es mi hija! Hizo muy bien. Dijo la verdad. Tú sabes que **los niños y los locos dicen las verdades.**

—A mí me dio mucha pena. La gente seguramente pensó que yo le había dicho a la niña que me pidiera el asiento.

—No te preocupes, la gente sabe que **los niños son muy sinceros y dicen lo que sienten.**

24 El diente miente, la cana engaña, pero la arruga no ofrece duda

(the tooth lies, the gray hair fools, but the wrinkle offers no doubt)
you can't turn back the clock

—He decidido que me voy a hacer la cirugía plástica. Ya tengo 55 años y no me gusta lucir viejo. Mi mujer es 20 años menor que yo. No quiero que la gente piense que es mi hija. Tú sabes que **el diente miente, la cana engaña, pero la arruga no ofrece duda.**

—No seas tonto. Está bien que cuides tu apariencia, pero una cirugía plástica es muy cara.

—Es que no quiero lucir viejo.

—**No es bueno esconder la edad.** Es mejor asumir los años que uno tiene.

25 El que no oye consejo no llega a viejo

(he who hears no advice will not get old)
advice when most needed is least heeded

—Mi padre me advirtió que no comprara una motocicleta, que son peligrosas y no muy prácticas.

—¿Y qué hiciste?

—Bueno, me compré la moto de todas maneras porque tenía muchas ganas de tenerla.

—¿Qué dijo tu padre cuando se enteró?

—No mucho. Me miró muy serio, sacudió la cabeza y dijo: **El que no oye consejo no llega a viejo.**

—Tiene razón. **Los consejos de los viejos nos ayudan a protegernos en la vida.** Hay muchos accidentes de motocicleta. Si yo fuera tú, la vendería y me compraría un carro, como dice tu padre.

26 Árbol que nace torcido jamás su tronco endereza

(tree that grows bent never straightens its trunk)

as the twig is bent, so is the tree inclined

—¡Ay, Gladys! ¡Mi hijo me tiene loca!

—¿Qué pasa? ¿Se porta mal?

—El problema es que le gusta quitarle los juguetes a sus hermanos, pero no prestar los suyos. Si alguien le toca sus juguetes se pone a patalear. No quiero tener un hijo así, egoísta.

—Bueno, pues trata de enseñarle a compartir sus cosas. Tú sabes que eso es difícil, pues **árbol que nace torcido jamás su tronco endereza.**

—Tú vas a ver que conmigo va a aprender. Dicen que **cada uno tiene su manera de ser desde que nace y que no se puede cambiar.** Pero a mi hijo yo lo voy a corregir.

Section Three

La verdad y la sabiduría

Truth and Knowledge

27 Hombre prevenido vale por dos

(a warned man is worth two)
forewarned is forearmed

—¿En qué piensas, Sergio?

—Tengo un poco de dinero ahorrado y lo quiero invertir en algún negocio. Estaba pensando comprar acciones en una compañía de computadoras.

—Ten cuidado; mira que la economía no está en muy buena situación. ¿No has leído el periódico?

—Sí, pero también he leído que a algunas compañías de computadoras les va muy bien.

—Piensa bien lo que haces con tu dinero. Recuerda que **hombre prevenido vale por dos.**

—Tienes razón, ya me informé. Sé exactamente cuáles son las compañías buenas para invertir y cuáles son las malas. **Es una gran ventaja actuar con cuidado** en los negocios.

28 Piensa el ladrón que todos son de su condición

(the thief thinks that all are of his condition)
there is no honor among thieves

—¡Estoy furiosa! Acabo de venir del supermercado. El dueño hizo que me detuvieran al salir para revisar mi bolsa. ¡Qué falta de respeto! Es la segunda vez que me tratan como si fuera una ladrona.

—Eso es un insulto. A mí me hicieron lo mismo la semana pasada. Ese dueño es muy desconfiado.

—Lo que pasa es que no es una persona honesta. Cobra precios muy altos. Quien nos está robando es él a todos nosotros. Y ya tú sabes: **piensa el ladrón que todos son de su condición.**

—Por eso es que el dueño trata mal a sus clientes. **La persona deshonesta piensa que todo el mundo es también deshonesto.**

—Pues conmigo cometió un error muy grave. Jamás voy a volver a comprar en ese supermercado.

29 El hábito no hace al monje

(the habit does not make the monk)
clothes do not make the man

—Tenemos que aconsejar a nuestra amiga Isabel.

—¿Qué problema tiene?

—Está buscando novio. Y dice que quiere un novio con alguna profesión y con dinero, que sólo vista traje y corbata.

—Ya veo. Isabel debería saber que **el hábito no hace al monje.**

—Claro que no. Mucha gente profesional no viste de traje y corbata. **No se puede juzgar a la gente por su forma de vestir.** Hay que conocer a cada persona para saber cómo es.

—Y también hay hombres que se gastan el poco dinero que tienen en vestir bien y ni ganan mucho ni tienen profesión.

30 El que ríe último ríe mejor

(he who last laughs, laughs better)
he who laughs last, laughs best

—¿Viste lo que le pasó a Nelson?

—Sí, le pusieron una multa por exceso de velocidad en la carretera.

—¿Te acuerdas que siempre se burlaba de mi manera de manejar? Decía que yo manejaba demasiado despacio y que era demasiado precavida. Me veía en el timón y se echaba a reír.

—Pero mira ahora, te puedes sentir satisfecha. **El que ríe último ríe mejor.**

—Me alegro de que le hayan puesto una multa. Así aprenderá a no excederse de velocidad. **Aunque se burlaba de mí, ahora verá que él estaba equivocado y que yo tengo la razón.**

31 Quien nada sabe, de nada duda

(who knows nothing, doubts nothing)
he that knows nothing, doubts nothing

[Efraín está convencido de que hay seres vivos en la luna.]

—Esther, ayer vi un programa en la televisión sobre los seres que viven en la luna.

—No es posible, Efraín. En la luna no hay vida.

—Pues yo lo vi con mis propios ojos.

—¿No sabes que en la luna no hay agua ni oxígeno? El agua y el oxígeno son necesarios para la vida.

—Bueno yo no sé si hay o no hay oxígeno, pero yo sí vi a los que habitan en la luna.

—Veo que efectivamente no sabes nada. Y **quien nada sabe, de nada duda.**

—¿Por qué me dices eso?

—Porque **las personas que no están informadas pueden creer cualquier cosa.** ¿Sabías también que el mundo es plano?

32 Quien estudia y no aprende, si no es asno lo parece

(who studies and does not learn, if he is not a donkey, he looks like one)
send a donkey to Paris, and he will return no wiser than he went

---

—Ana María, ¿qué te pareció Carlos?

—Me parece simpático, pero no muy inteligente.

—¿Por qué dices eso?

—Virginia es compañera de clase de él. Me ha dicho que Carlos siempre está estudiando, pero saca muy malas calificaciones. Y ya sabes que **quien estudia y no aprende, si no es asno lo parece.**

—¡Pobre Carlos! No me gusta que se burlen de él. Es verdad que **no es muy inteligente, pues estudia mucho y no aprende.** Pero es muy buena persona, muy chistoso y alegre.

33 De noche todos los gatos son pardos

(at night all cats are brown)
all cats are gray in the dark

—Berta, anoche un señor tocó a la puerta. Me fijé por la ventana y me pareció que era mi cuñado Armando. Tú sabes, **de noche todos los gatos son pardos.**

—Sí, es cierto que **en la oscuridad no se distinguen bien las personas.** ¿Y qué pasó? ¿No era Armando?

—¡No, qué va! Cuando encendí la luz para abrir la puerta, me di cuenta que era un hombre desconocido. Lo bueno es que no alcancé a abrirle la puerta. Nos miramos por un instante por la ventanilla de la puerta, y él se mostró muy sorprendido. Dio un paso atrás, mirando detenidamente la casa y el domicilio. Luego se disculpó muy amablemente por la molestia y se alejó.

—No me digas que se equivocó de casa.

—¡Sí, así es! Parece que de noche también todas las casas son iguales, ¿verdad?

34 Mucho hablar y poco decir juntos suelen ir

**(talking much and saying little
usually go together)**
empty vessels make the most noise

[Patricia y Ramón hablan del nuevo hombre que ha entrado a trabajar en la compañía.]

—¿Te has fijado cómo habla el nuevo? —dice Patricia.

—Sí. Lo juzga todo, de todo sabe y no está de acuerdo con la opinión de nadie —dice Ramón.

—Y no para de hablar.

—No para. Ya lo dice mi mujer: **Mucho hablar y poco decir juntos suelen ir.**

—El ejemplo perfecto de eso lo tenemos ahora aquí. Creo que el nuevo quiere hacer una buena impresión.

—Pues su forma de actuar tiene el efecto contrario. **Cuando una persona habla mucho es para ocultar su ignorancia.**

—Cuidado, ahí viene. Bueno, me voy a mi escritorio para no oírlo hablar.

40

35 Unos dicen lo que saben y otros saben lo que dicen

(some say what they know and others know what they say)
the greatest scholars are not the best preachers

—Ese programa de televisión a mí no me convence. Ese hombre dice que es un psíquico y que ha estudiado las estrellas y que sabe mucho de astrología y demás. Pero no creo que sepa mucho de nada.

—Tienes razón, **unos dicen lo que saben y otros saben lo que dicen.**

—Yo prefiero ver programas con psicólogos o sociólogos que explican cómo se comporta la gente y por qué. **Las personas que tienen conocimientos de verdad, los comparten sin hacer alarde de saber mucho.**

36 Ojos que no ven, corazón que no siente

(eyes that do not see, heart that does not feel)
what the eye doesn't see, the heart doesn't grieve over

[Las dos vecinas conversan a través de las rejas de los patios respectivos de sus casas.]

—María, tú sabes que a Laura le gusta hablar mal de ti. El otro día le tuve que decir: "Mira, Laura, María es mi vecina, es muy buena persona y no quiero que me hables mal de ella."

—Gracias, pero, ¿tú sabes qué? **Ojos que no ven, corazón que no siente.**

—Claro. Pero, bueno, quería que tú supieras que ella es quien está hablando mal de ti.

—Te lo agradezco, pero prefiero no saber nada de eso. **Lo que uno no ve con sus propios ojos ni escucha con sus propios oídos, no le hace daño.** Gracias por tu preocupación, pero tengo cosas más importantes que hacer en lugar de preocuparme por ser amiga de todo el mundo.

37 Al César lo que es del César y a Dios lo que es de Dios

(to Caesar what belongs to Caesar and to God what belongs to God)
give credit where credit is due

—Dime, Lidia, ¿cómo está tu hermano? Hace tiempo que no me hablas de él.

—Está bien, como siempre. No tiene trabajo todavía. Dice que quiere ser pintor. Se pasa el día en su cuarto pintando óleos. Estoy cansada del olor a pintura.

—¿Crees que es buen pintor?

—Eso sí, **al César lo que es del César y a Dios lo que es de Dios.** Mi hermano tendrá muchos defectos, pero sí es buen pintor. Sus cuadros son maravillosos. Yo creo que un día tendrá éxito.

—**¡Qué bueno que sabes reconocer el mérito en los demás!** ¿Y tienes talento de pintora también?

—¿Yo? ¡No, en lo absoluto! Yo no me parezco en nada a mi hermano. ¡Voy a ser científica!

38 Aprendiz de todo y maestro de nada

(apprentice of all and master of nothing)
jack of all trades, master of none

[Dos amigos conversan en el patio de la escuela, durante el descanso.]

—¿Oíste a Pedro?

—Sí, de nuevo con lo mismo.

—Dice que va a estudiar idiomas, computación y, después, medicina.

—Ése va a ser como dice mi tío: **aprendiz de todo y maestro de nada.**

—Cierto. Va a ser un aficionado en las tres cosas. Al final, ni va a hablar bien los idiomas ni va a dominar la computadora.

—Y lo que soy yo, ni loco me voy a consultar con él ni para un dolor de callos.

—Y yo menos. **El que quiere aprender muchas cosas al mismo tiempo, no aprende ninguna bien.**

39 Vale más una imagen que mil palabras

(better an image than a thousand words)
a picture is worth a thousand words

—Marina, ¿cómo te fue en el juicio hoy?

—Estupendamente. Afortunadamente, tenía fotos del accidente para demostrarle al juez que mi cliente era inocente.

—¿Y qué hizo el otro abogado?

—El otro abogado tenía muchos papeles. Pero tú sabes que **vale más una imagen que mil palabras.** Gané mi caso.

—Entonces es cierto que **a veces una buena fotografía es la mejor explicación.**

40 Vale más una verdad amarga que muchas mentiras dulces

(better a bitter truth than many sweet lies)
honesty is the best policy

—Santiago, tengo que confesarte una cosa.

—Dime, Irene, ¿por qué estás tan seria, mi amor?

—Es que no estoy enamorada de ti.

—¿Cómo? ¿Estás bromeando?

—No estoy bromeando. **Vale más una verdad amarga que muchas mentiras dulces.** Tú eres muy bueno, pero yo no estoy enamorada de ti.

—¿Por qué no me lo dijiste antes?

—No quería herirte los sentimientos, pero mi madre me aconsejó que **es mejor decir la verdad, aunque duela, en lugar de mentir.**

41 El saber no ocupa lugar

(knowledge does not occupy space)
knowledge is power

—Paco, acabas de terminar el curso de francés y ahora me dices que vas a empezar el de japonés. ¿No te cansas de tanto estudiar?

—No, Micaela. A mí me gusta estudiar.

—Pero, ¿por qué estudias idiomas? ¡Le tienes miedo a los aviones! Nunca vas a visitar los países donde se hablan. En serio, Paco, yo no te entiendo.

—Eso no importa. **El saber no ocupa lugar.** Aunque yo nunca vaya a esos países, tal vez consiga un trabajo donde haga falta hablar diferentes idiomas. **Siempre es bueno saber más.** Uno nunca sabe cuándo los conocimientos pueden hacer falta.

42 No hay tonto, por tonto que sea, que tonto se crea

(there is no fool, no matter how much a fool, who believes himself a fool)
no fool thinks he's a fool

—José acaba de descalificar para la competencia de mañana porque se le olvidó llenar el cuestionario. ¡Qué tontería ha cometido!

—No puedo creer que se le haya olvidado. Yo se lo recordé varias veces. Siempre me decía que sí, que lo iba a hacer.

—Pues, no lo hizo. Y hoy me dice que no fue culpa suya, que él no sabía que había que llenar un cuestionario.

—Claro, es que **no hay tonto, por tonto que sea, que tonto se crea.**

—Es cierto. **A nadie le gusta admitir su falta de inteligencia.**

Section Four

El amor y la amistad

Love and Friendship

43 Antes que te cases, mira lo que haces

(before you marry, look at what you do)
look before you leap

—El contrato es sólo por dos años y es muy ventajoso.

—Sí, ya lo sé. Pero tendrás que vivir todo ese tiempo en un país extranjero, en una cultura extraña a la tuya. Eso es como contraer matrimonio y mira, como dice mi madre: **antes que te cases, mira lo que haces.**

—Es verdad, voy a pensarlo un poco más.

—**Antes de tomar una decisión importante, considera bien lo que vas a hacer.** Tómate tu tiempo para eso. No analices sólo las ganancias, analiza también las pérdidas.

—Sí. Si me voy a trabajar allá, por supuesto que me separo de mis padres y de mis amigos... Sí, voy a pensarlo mejor. Tengo un mes para decidirlo. Gracias por la advertencia.

44 En la unión está la fuerza

(in union is the strength)
in unity there's strength

—Hace rato que no nos suben el sueldo en este trabajo. Si queremos que nos lo suban tenemos que unirnos.

—¿Tú crees que el dueño de la compañía nos va a hacer caso?

—¡Claro que sí! **En la unión está la fuerza.** Todos los trabajadores nos tenemos que unir. Ya sabemos que si estamos divididos no lograremos nada, pero **si estamos unidos, podremos tener éxito.**

—Muy buena idea. Vamos a tener una reunión esta tarde, después del trabajo. Hace falta que todos los trabajadores vengan. Tenemos que hacer una petición todos juntos. Es la única manera de mejorar esta situación.

45 Haz bien y no mires a quién

(do good and do not look to whom)
a good deed is never lost

—¿Por qué le diste dinero a ese hombre en la calle? ¿No sabes que es un vago sinvergüenza?

—Bueno, lo vi muy pobre y me pidió dinero. ¿Qué iba a hacer? Yo siempre pienso: **Haz bien y no mires a quién.**

—Pero no está bien darle dinero a alguien que no trabaja y pasa todo el tiempo pidiendo en la calle.

—Yo trato de no juzgar a la gente. Yo pienso que si alguien está necesitado, **uno debe prestarle ayuda sin preguntar nada ni imponer condiciones.**

—No sé si en realidad has hecho un bien o un mal.

46 Si a tu vecino quieres conocer, averigua qué libros suele leer

(if you want to know your neighbor, find out what books he usually reads)

know your neighbor from the books he reads

—Nuestro vecino es muy raro. No habla mucho. Se pasa el día en la casa leyendo.

—¿Nunca has hablado con él?

—No. Parece que trabaja de noche, pero no sabemos qué hace.

—Bueno, **si a tu vecino quieres conocer, averigua qué libros suele leer.**

—Tú lo has dicho, **los libros que lee una persona son una buena indicación de sus valores y forma de ser.** Y ¿sabes qué? ¡Creo que nuestro vecino es un asesino! Siempre está leyendo novelas de misterio policiaco.

—¡No me hagas reír! Mi hermano conoce a tu vecino. Tu vecino no es un asesino. ¡Es policía y trabaja de noche!

47 En martes, ni te cases ni te embarques

(on Tuesday neither marry nor embark)
never marry or take a trip on Tuesday

—Joaquín, me dieron la buena noticia de que Ileana y tú se van a casar.

—Sí, el mes que viene va a ser un año que nos conocemos. Ese mismo día nos vamos a casar, al año exacto de habernos conocido.

—¿Harán la boda un sábado?

—No, la fecha cae en martes. Queremos casarnos ese día porque es una fecha muy importante para nosotros.

—Oye, eso no es buena idea. Dicen los sabios que **en martes, ni te cases ni te embarques.**

—Ésa es una superstición vieja y yo no creo en ella. No es cierto que **es de mala suerte casarse o salir de viaje en martes.** No te voy a hacer caso. Ileana y yo nos vamos a casar ese día, diga lo que diga la gente. Ya está decidido. Ese mismo día salimos de luna de miel en un crucero por el mar Caribe. Y sé que seremos muy felices.

48 El amor es ciego

(love is blind)
love is blind

—¿Sabes que Carmen y Julio se van a casar?

—Son novios desde hace dos años. ¿Verdad?

—Sí, pero los dos son personas muy egoístas y desordenadas. Julio nunca tiene un trabajo fijo y siempre sale a pasear con sus amigos en lugar de sacar a Carmen. Y Carmen, en lugar de hablar con él, es muy conflictiva con sus amigos. Pero dicen que están muy enamorados y se quieren casar.

—Ni Julio es el marido ideal, ni Carmen es la esposa ideal. ¡La verdad es que **el amor es ciego!**

—Sí, parece que **se quieren tanto que no se ven los defectos uno del otro.**

—Bueno, mi amiga, si algún día me ves en la misma situación, lista para casarme con alguien que no me conviene, por favor, dímelo. No quiero cometer el mismo error que Carmen.

—Te lo prometo, amiga.

49 Amor con amor se paga

(love with love is paid)
one good turn deserves another

—Julia es la mejor supervisora que he tenido en la vida. Ésa es la verdad.

—Te doy la razón. Siempre está atenta a cualquier problema que podamos tener y hasta nos pregunta por la familia. Es excepcional.

—Por eso la gente la quiere tanto aquí en la compañía.

—Es que **amor con amor se paga.** Es así.

—Es como una ley universal. Como la de la gravedad o alguna otra de esas leyes físicas. En este caso es la ley del amor. **Si entregas amor, vas a recibir amor.** Se cumple siempre.

50 Cada quien con su cada cual

(each one with his each one)
birds of a feather flock together

—Rogelio, te invito a ver el partido de fútbol el domingo. Tengo dos entradas.

—No gracias, los domingos prefiero pasarlos con mi amigo el mecánico. Así lo ayudo y yo aprendo también. Tú sabes que a mí me gusta mucho la mecánica.

—Yo creo que es más divertido ir a un partido de fútbol, pero bueno, **cada quien con su cada cual.**

—Invita a Néstor. A él sí le gusta mucho el fútbol. Él irá contigo.

Las personas que tienen los mismos gustos o intereses buscan la manera de juntarse.

51 Con los años vienen los desengaños

(with the years come the disappointments)
familiarity breeds contempt

[Adela se queja de su marido con su amiga Lola. Su amiga le contesta:]

—Me asombra oírte. ¿No repetías siempre que Pablito era el hombre más cariñoso, más inteligente y capaz del planeta? ¿Adónde se han ido los elogios?

—Imagínatelo —dice Adela en tono triste—. **Con los años vienen los desengaños.**

—¿Te has dado cuenta? **Con el tiempo, podemos ver las faltas de la gente.** Con los maridos es igual. La boda y los primeros años son un sueño, pero después viene la realidad. ¿Por qué será que cuando nos casamos pensamos que todo será siempre como la luna de miel?

—No sé. Pero la verdad es que fue un error casarme con mi marido. Ya no somos felices.

52 El que anda con lobos, a aullar se enseña

(he who walks with wolves learns to howl)
if you lie down with dogs, you'll get up
with fleas

—Rogelio, no me gustan esos nuevos amigos que tienes. ¿De dónde han salido? ¿Qué hacen?

—No te preocupes, papá, yo sé quiénes son mis amigos.

—Ten cuidado, hijo, mira que **el que anda con lobos, a aullar se enseña.**

—Ya sé, ya me lo has dicho muchas veces.

—Pues no me voy a cansarte de decírtelo. **Las personas se influyen mutuamente.** No quiero que vayas a tener ningún problema.

—Ya sé, ya sé. La verdad es que los conozco desde hace poco, pero no te preocupes. Voy a estar alerta. ¿Tienes confianza en tu hijo o no?

53 No hay mejor hermano que un buen vecino al lado

(there is no better brother than a good neighbor next door)
good neighbors are hard to find

—Hace veinte años que vivimos en esta casa. Los vecinos de al lado también ocuparon su casa hace veinte años.

—¿Son buenos amigos?

—Somos más que amigos. Tú sabes que **no hay mejor hermano que un buen vecino al lado.** Somos como familia. Nos visitamos y nos ayudamos cuando hay necesidad.

—Tuviste suerte, no todo el mundo tiene buenos vecinos. **Cuando el vecino es bueno, es como tener a alguien de la familia al lado.**

54 Dime con quién andas y te diré quién eres

(tell me who you go with and I'll tell you who you are)

a man is known by the company he keeps

—Omar, ¿sabes que estás tomando fama de tramposo y mentiroso?

—¿Yo? ¿Por qué?

—Porque tu mejor amigo, Rubén, estaba haciendo trampa en el examen de historia. Todo el mundo pensaba que era estudioso, pero resultó ser un tramposo.

—Pero yo sí soy estudioso.

—La gente decía lo mismo de Rubén antes. Y como ustedes dos siempre andan juntos... Tú sabes lo que piensa la gente: **dime con quién andas y te diré quién eres.**

—Sí, yo sé que **la gente piensa que uno es igual que sus amigos.**

—Bueno, pues si quieres cuidar tu reputación como buen estudiante, no seas tan amigo de un tramposo como Rubén. Busca la amistad de otros estudiantes honestos como tú.

55 El amigo lo escojo yo, el pariente no

(the friend I choose, the relative, no)
select your friend with a silk-gloved hand

—Carlos, me dijeron que andas siempre con Alberto y Matías. ¿Es verdad?

—Y... ¿por qué me lo preguntas?

—Todo el mundo sabe que ésos siempre andan en líos. No me parece buena idea que seas amigo de ellos.

—Jorge, tú eres mi hermano mayor, pero eso no te da derecho a escoger a mis amigos. Además, la gente no habla muy bien de ti tampoco, por si no lo sabías.

—Ay, Carlitos, ¿Nunca oíste el refrán: **El amigo lo escojo yo, el pariente no?**

—Ésos son dichos de gente mayor, Jorge. Además, ¿qué quiere decir?

—Que no se puede escoger la familia, pero a los amigos sí. Por lo tanto, **se debe usar buen criterio al escoger amigos.** A propósito, ¿quieres saber por qué la gente habla mal de mí? Porque hace mucho tiempo anduve en malas compañías y a nadie se le ha olvidado todavía.

56 Más vale malo conocido que bueno por conocer

(better bad known than good yet to know)
better the devil you know than the devil you don't know

—Nancy, ¿ya cambiaste de peluquero?

—No, todavía. Sigo con el mismo que me quemó el pelo la última vez que me hice un permanente.

—¿Cómo es posible? Me dijiste que después de lo que te hizo en el pelo lo odiabas y nunca más volverías a él.

—Sí, eso fue lo que te dije, Violeta. Pero mi peluquero me prometió arreglarme el pelo gratis dos veces más para compensar por su error. Hace mucho tiempo que voy a él. Ya él conoce mis gustos y me cobra barato. Pensé, bueno, **más vale malo conocido que bueno por conocer.** Así que lo perdoné.

—Te entiendo, a veces **es mejor cuidar lo que uno tiene, aunque no sea perfecto, que exponerse a cambiarlo por algo mejor y salir perdiendo.**

Section Five
La adversidad
Adversity

57 No hay mal que por bien no venga

(there's no evil that does not bring some good)
every cloud has a silver lining

—¡Qué lástima! No tienen helado de chocolate.

—¿Por qué no pides otro sabor?

—El único helado que me gusta es el de chocolate. No importa. Ahora que lo pienso, es mejor así. **No hay mal que por bien no venga.**

—¿Por qué dices eso?

—Es que estoy muy gordo. Si sigo comiendo tanto helado de chocolate me voy a poner más gordo todavía. **A veces lo que parece ser un problema es en realidad una ayuda.**

—Sí, es mejor tener una actitud positiva y verle la parte buena a todo.

58 El gato escaldado del agua fría huye

(the scalded cat flees from cold water)
once bitten twice shy

—Estamos formando un grupo para hacer un viaje en barco este domingo. ¿Quieres venir?

—¿Yo? ¡Jamás! Ya di un viaje en barco el año pasado y por poco me muero.

¿Qué pasó?

—El barco tenía un problema en el motor. Nos quedamos varados en medio del océano. Tuvimos que llamar al rescate por radio.

—Pero el barco en donde vamos el domingo es nuevo y el motor es excelente.

—No gracias, tú sabes que **el gato escaldado del agua fría huye.**

—Te comprendo. **El que ha tenido un susto muy grande se queda con miedo a todo.**

59 No hay que ahogarse en un vaso de agua

(one should not drown in a glass of water)
don't make a mountain out of a molehill

—¿Ya encontraste trabajo, Pedro?

—Nada. Me ofrecieron un trabajo, pero queda muy lejos de la casa y yo no tengo carro.

—¿No puedes tomar el autobús?

—El problema es que el autobús se demora mucho. Tendría que salir de la casa a las 6 de la mañana para llegar al trabajo a las 8. Todavía no les he contestado si voy a tomar el trabajo o no.

—Eso no es problema ninguno. **No hay que ahogarse en un vaso de agua.** Puedes tomar el autobús para llegar al trabajo. Y dentro de dos o tres meses te puedes comprar un carro con lo que ganes.

—Efectivamente, **mi problema no es tan grave.** Me hace falta tener un trabajo. Voy a decirles que sí y más adelante me compro un carro.

60 Perro ladrador, poco mordedor

(barking dog, bites little)
barking dogs seldom bite

—Lo que más me gusta de mi jefe es que siempre está peleando y regañándolo a uno.

—¿Y eso te gusta?

—Sí, este jefe que tenemos ahora grita y pelea cuando llego tarde, o cuando no le gusta algo, pero no nos hace nada. Tú sabes que **perro ladrador, poco mordedor.**

—Ya veo lo que dices. El jefe anterior nunca regañaba ni gritaba, pero era muy traicionero. A la hora de cobrar, te quitaba dinero por llegar tarde.

—Es lo que te digo. Este jefe nuestro es **alguien que grita y amenaza, pero no nos hace daño.**

—Así y todo, es mejor no abusar. Es verdad que no muerde, pero no sigas llegando tarde para que el jefe deje de ladrar. Esos ladridos del jefe no son agradables.

61 Amigo en la adversidad, es amigo de verdad

(a friend in adversity is a true friend)
a friend in need is a friend indeed

—¡Cómo ha llovido, Emilio!

—No me digas nada. Se inundó el sótano de mi casa. Ahora tengo que limpiarlo todo y quitar la alfombra. Es muchísimo trabajo.

—En mi casa no tuvimos problemas. Yo te voy a ayudar.

—No te preocupes. No te quiero molestar.

—No es ninguna molestia; para eso somos amigos, ¿no?

—Te lo voy a agradecer. **Amigo en la adversidad, es amigo de verdad.**

—Te ayudaré con mucho gusto. **Los amigos de verdad se ayudan cuando hay necesidad.**

62 El piso de uno es el techo de otro

(someone's floor is the ceiling for someone else)
one man's gravy is another man's poison

—Rodolfo, ¿es verdad que te quieres ir de tu trabajo?

—Sí, Raúl. Mi hermana me dio trabajo en su compañía. Pero la verdad es que no me gusta tanto como yo pensaba. Y me han ofrecido otro trabajo, pero no quiero quedar mal con mi hermana. A ella le hace falta un trabajador.

—Oye, Rodolfo. Yo estoy sin trabajo. ¿Por qué no le hablas a tu hermana de mí? Yo tomo tu puesto, así no quedas mal con ella y yo tendré trabajo.

—No es mala idea, Raúl. Dicen que **el piso de uno es el techo de otro.**

—Como ves, Rodolfo, **lo que es malo o incómodo para uno resulta ser bueno y cómodo para otro.**

—Te va a gustar el trabajo, Raúl. Además, mi hermana trata a todo el mundo bien, menos a su propio hermano.

63 A mal tiempo buena cara

(to bad weather, good face)
keep your chin up

—Siéntate, que tengo que darte una mala noticia.

—¿Qué pasa? Por la cara que tienes parece que se acabó el mundo.

—Acabo de quedarme sin trabajo.

—Bueno, ¿eso es todo? No es el fin del mundo.

—¿Te parece poco? No tengo trabajo.

—Ricardo, **a mal tiempo buena cara.** Con deprimirte y mortificarte no vas a lograr nada. **Lo mejor es enfrentar los problemas con ánimo alegre para poder superarlos.** Eso es todo lo que hay que tener. Así que levanta ese ánimo y sonríe. Te invito al cine. Ya mañana tendrás tiempo de buscar trabajo.

64 Donde una puerta se cierra, otra se abre

(where one door closes, another one opens)
when one door shuts, another opens

—Ya ves adónde me han llevado las deudas: a perder el carro, la casa en la playa, mi crédito. En fin, ¡estoy destruido!

—Quizás golpeado, pero no vencido. Sencillamente, tienes que aprender la lección y empezar de nuevo. **Donde una puerta se cierra, otra se abre.**

—¡Ah, no estoy para refranes viejos!

—No es un refrán, es una verdad. Yo he pasado por eso también. **Detrás de un problema grande siempre viene alguna ayuda o algo mejor.** Por eso te digo, toma esta oportunidad para organizar tus finanzas. Ponte en el buen camino. Vas a ver cómo tu vida se arregla.

65 Como el perro del hortelano, ni come ni deja comer

(like the farmer's dog, who neither eats nor allows others to eat)
misery loves company

[Tatiana habla por teléfono con su amiga Marta.]

—No vamos a la playa. José no quiere ir. O se hace el que no quiere ir. No sé.

—En ese caso, ven tú sola con el niño.

—No, dice que no debemos ir. Dice que si él se quiere quedar en la casa, no está bien que el niño y yo lo dejemos solo todo el domingo.

—¡Ay! Tu marido está **como el perro del hortelano: ni come ni deja comer.**

—Ése es su defecto. Siempre ha sido así, **ni hace lo que quiere hacer, ni deja que los demás hagan lo que quieran.**

—Pero ya esos tiempos pasaron, mi amiga. ¡Por favor!

—Es verdad. Espérame, salgo para allá con el niño. Creo que hoy es un buen día para darle una lección a ese esposo mío.

66 Todo tiene solución, menos la muerte

(everything has a solution, except death)
nothing is certain but death and taxes

[Elena llama a su esposa, Alejandro, al trabajo para decirle que su hija Luisita acaba de suspender otra asignatura.]

—¿Por qué me llamas al trabajo con tanta urgencia?

—¿Te parece poco? Ésta es la segunda asignatura que suspende Luisita. Esta hija tuya me va a matar de disgustos. Así no va a llegar a nada en la vida.

—Mi hija sola no, es tu hija también. Y vamos, que no es para tanto. **Todo tiene solución, menos la muerte.** Vamos a conseguirle un maestro particular para que la ayude a hacer las tareas en la casa. Eso le va a mostrar cómo estudiar mejor y sacar buenas notas. **El problema no es tan grave.**

—Ojalá que ésa sea la solución.

67 Quien siembra vientos recoge tempestades

(he who sows winds will reap tempests)
you reap what you sow

[La abuela conversa con su nieta mayor. La nieta quiere vengarse de su amiga por hablar mal de ella.]

—No creo que debas pensar en vengarte de tu amiga. ¿Qué ganas con todo eso?

—¿Qué gano? Nada menos que vengarme de ella, por todo lo que me ha hecho. ¿Te parece poco? Me la va a pagar de todas formas. Ahora yo soy quien va a hablar mal de Susana y regar rumores.

—Hija, hija, eso no está bien. **Quien siembra vientos recoge tempestades.** Aprende a perdonar. Lo que pasó, pasó. **Si haces un mal, o siembras odio, vas a recibir otros males y más odio.**

—No lo creo. Pero, además, no me interesa. Lo que quiero es vengarme de Susana por hablar mal de mí.

—Piensa bien lo que haces. Yo, por mi parte, he cumplido con darte un consejo.

68 Más vale precaver que tener que lamentar

(better to prevent than to have to lament)
better safe than sorry

—Ayer, cuando salí, llevé el paraguas pero no llovió. Hoy voy a dejar el paraguas. Es una molestia llevarlo a todas partes. Además, tengo la preocupación de perderlo.

—Mira, alégrate si no llovió ayer. Pero creo que hoy sí va a llover. Debes llevar el paraguas. Recuerda que **más vale precaver que tener que lamentar.**

—Sí, **es preferible una molestia pequeña antes de tener que afrontarse a una molestia más grande después.** Llevar el paraguas a todas partes no es agradable, pero mojarse es peor.

—A mí siempre me pasa lo mismo; cuando llevo el paraguas no llueve. Pero cada vez que lo dejo en la casa cae tremendo aguacero.

—Pues me llevo el paraguas y si se me pierde, te puedo echar la culpa a ti.

69 Casa sin madre, río sin cauce

(a house without a mother, a river without a course)
the woman is the key of the house

—Liliana, ¿es verdad que la presidenta de la universidad tuya renunció?

—Sí, desgraciadamente así es. Hace ya tres semanas y no han encontrado a nadie que la reemplace.

—Me han dicho que las cosas por allá andan como **casa sin madre, río sin cauce.**

—Exactamente. Desde su renuncia, los asuntos de la universidad son **un caos total porque no hay dirección.**

—Es una lástima, porque ella era una estupenda presidenta. ¿Y dónde trabaja ahora?

—Pues... ¡se fue a escalar el Everest! Dijo que estaba cansada de tanto trabajo y tanta organización.

—¡Caramba!

70 Uno siembra y el otro siega

one plants, the other one reaps)
you should not reap the benefits of someone
else's labor

—Carla, estoy enojadísima contigo. ¿Quién trabajó más en recaudar fondos para la nueva biblioteca? ¿Tú o yo?

—Pues... claro que... tú, Tina.

—Entonces, ¿por qué aparece tu nombre en este artículo como la persona principal?

—El periodista se... ¡habrá equivocado! Sí, seguro que eso fue lo que pasó. Yo le di tu nombre y el mío, te lo juro.

—Esto es increíble. **Uno siembra y el otro siega.** Me pasé todo el año trabajando, pero **tú te aprovechaste de mis esfuerzos.**

—Lo siento, Tina.

—Más lo siento yo, Carla. Acabas de perder a una buena amiga.

71 Al mejor escribano se le va un borrón

(even the best writer slips up with a smudge)
nobody's perfect

—¿Te gustó la película?

—Tiene muy buen argumento. Y Regina es mi actriz favorita. Pero me parece que en algunas escenas ella no actuó muy bien.

—Ella es muy buena actriz, pero bueno, **al mejor escribano se le va un borrón.**

—Como es mi actriz favorita, soy un poco exigente con ella. Yo sé que **nadie es perfecto,** pero me hago la ilusión de que ella sí lo es. Por eso no me gusta verla actuar mal.

—Bueno, ya que sabes tanto de actuación, escríbele una carta con todos tus consejos.

72 A un gustazo, un trancazo

(to a pleasure, a blow with a club)
after the feast comes the reckoning

—Mamá, ¿tienes algo para el dolor de estómago? Me siento muy mal.

—Te advertí que no comieras tanta pizza. **A un gustazo, un trancazo.** Ahora no te quejes.

—Tienes razón, **disfruté demasiado y ahora estoy pagando las consecuencias.**

—Bueno, te voy a traer un poco de bicarbonato con agua. Pronto te sentirás mejor.

Section Six

Hacer las cosas

Getting Things Done

73 Más vale tarde que nunca

(later is more valuable than never)
better late than never

—¡Al fin llegaste, Miguel! Todos estábamos preocupados.

—Discúlpenme por llegar tan tarde a este almuerzo. No conozco esta zona y me perdí un poco por el camino. No encontraba el restaurante.

—No te preocupes. **Más vale tarde que nunca.**

—Gracias, Marta. Yo también pensé que **es mejor llegar, aunque sea tarde, que no llegar.**

—Ya nosotros pedimos, pero como ves, no hemos empezado a comer todavía. Nos demoramos en pedir para darte tiempo a llegar.

—Gracias por esperar. Voy a pedir ahora mismo.

—Apúrate. Seguro que tienes tanta hambre como nosotros.

74 No por mucho madrugar amanece más temprano

(not for getting up early will the day start earlier)
for the early riser the dawn comes not the sooner

—Ya lo tengo todo preparado para el viaje a Argentina.

—¿Cuándo te vas, mañana?

—No, el mes que viene. Pero ya lo tengo todo listo. Lo malo es que algunas de las cosas que guardé en la maleta me hacen falta. Y tengo que abrir las maletas a cada rato para sacar algo.

—Yo creo que has preparado tus maletas con demasiado anticipo. **No por mucho madrugar amanece más temprano.**

—Es cierto que **no vale la pena tomar prevenciones exageradas, pues no siempre da resultado.** Pero es que tengo tantas ganas de irme de viaje que no pude resistir la tentación de hacer las maletas.

75 No dejes para mañana lo que puedas hacer hoy

(don't leave for tomorrow what you can do today)
don't put off for tomorrow what you can do today

—¿Qué pasa, Carlos? Ayer te llamé por teléfono, pero tu línea está desconectada. ¿Hay algún problema?

—El problema soy yo, Susana. Siempre me atraso con los pagos. Cuando me llega la cuenta del teléfono, la pongo a un lado y me olvido de ella.

—Hace tres meses te pasó lo mismo. Siempre dejas las cosas para más tarde. **¡No dejes para mañana lo que puedas hacer hoy!**

—Tienes razón, no debo atrasarme en hacer las cosas. **Lo mejor es hacerlas lo más pronto posible.** Cuando me atraso, siempre tengo problemas.

—Sí, es mejor hacer las cosas a tiempo para vivir más tranquilo.

76 Una golondrina no hace el verano

(one swallow does not make the summer)
one swallow does not a summer make

—Luisa, ayer mi equipo ganó la primera competencia de natación del año. ¡Vamos a ganar el campeonato este año!

—No vayas tan de prisa, Marta, **una golondrina no hace el verano.**

—¿Qué me quieres decir con eso? ¿No confías de que nuestro equipo ganará el campeonato?

—No es que no confíe, sino que **un solo ejemplo no es suficiente para decidirlo todo.** Si de verdad quieren ganar, sigan entrenándose.

—Yo no sé de cuentos de golondrinas. Lo que sí te digo es que nosotras somos las mejores. Y golondrinas o no, ¡vamos a ganar!

77 La experiencia es la madre de la ciencia

(experience is the mother of science)
experience is the mother of science

[En la clase de diseño gráfico, el profesor termina de dar la clase y dice:]

—Ahora, tienen un par de meses para practicar estos dos programas de computación en el laboratorio. Eso es esencial. Recuerden que **la experiencia es la madre de la ciencia.**

—Profesor, pero nosotros queremos ser diseñadores gráficos, no científicos —responde un estudiante.

—Te crees muy chistoso, ¿verdad? Lo que quiero decir es que **si practican, tendrán la experiencia para hacer un buen trabajo.** Así que vayan para el laboratorio a practicar, y llegarán a ser buenos diseñadores gráficos.

78 Del dicho al hecho hay largo trecho

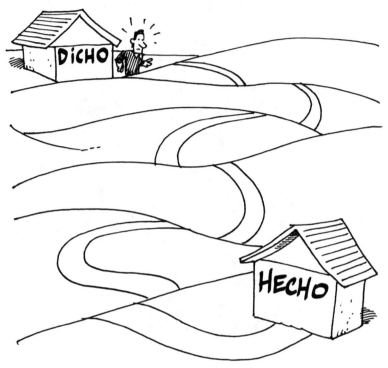

(from said to done there is a long way)
easier said than done

—Sigo con problemas con Alejandro —le dice Ana a su madre.

—¿Cuál es el problema ahora?

—Quiere que deje mi trabajo y que me quede en la casa todo el santo día.

—¿Pero y eso qué cosa es?

—¡Ay, mami! Tú sabes que él siempre ha sido muy machista. Dice que si no dejo de trabajar para el mes que viene, se va de la casa y me deja sola.

—Eso es un cuento, hija. **Del dicho al hecho hay largo trecho.**

—¿Tú crees?

—Mira, eso es sólo para asustarte. **Es fácil decir que uno va a hacer algo, pero es más difícil hacerlo.** Muéstrate tranquila y firme. Habla con él para que cambie ese machismo. ¿Dónde se cree tu marido que está viviendo? ¿En la época de las cavernas?

79 Quien tiene lengua, a Roma llega

(Who has a tongue, gets to Rome)
ask and you shall receive

—Fernando, ¿cómo hiciste para que tu madre te prestara el carro?

—Tú me conoces, y sabes que **quien tiene lengua, a Roma llega.**

—¿Hablaste con ella para convencerla?

—Claro que sí; **para lograr algo hay que saber hablar y convencer a los demás.** Le expliqué que me hacía mucha falta tener el carro. Le prometí que lo iba a llenar de gasolina y que me ocuparía de lavarlo el resto del mes. Tanto le hablé y le prometí, que accedió a mi deseo.

80 Quien mucho abarca, poco aprieta

(who spreads out too much squeezes little)
don't spread yourself too thin

—Vicente, ayer conseguí otro trabajo. Empiezo el sábado.

—Pero, Consuelo, entonces, ¿dejas la universidad?

—No, qué va. El trabajo nuevo es en una tienda, sólo los fines de semana.

—Entonces, ¿vas a dejar tu trabajo habitual en la oficina? ¿O vas a dejar tus juegos de baloncesto los domingos?

—No, tampoco.

—Creo que estás loca. ¿Cuándo vas a descansar? ¿Cuándo vas a tener tiempo para estudiar?

—Los sábados por la noche.

—Te digo que estás loca. **Quien mucho abarca, poco aprieta.** Ni vas a estudiar bien, ni vas a dormir bien, ni vas a trabajar correctamente.

—Mis padres me dicen lo mismo. Dicen que **quien trata de hacer muchas cosas a la vez, no tiene tiempo para hacer ninguna bien.** Pero yo les digo que yo sí puedo. Soy joven y tengo mucha energía.

81 Camarón que se duerme, se lo lleva la corriente

(the current carries off the shrimp that falls asleep)
don't rest on your laurels

—¿Qué tal, Olga? ¿Cómo le va a tu hijo con los estudios?

—Le va muy bien. Cada año toma uno o dos cursos. Dice que no tiene prisa y que así puede estudiar mejor.

—Pues, mi hija ya va a terminar. Y seguro que encontrará un buen trabajo antes que tu hijo. Dile a tu hijo que se apure, que **camarón que se duerme, se lo lleva la corriente.**

—Tienes razón, yo sé que **el que no se apura, se queda atrás.** Pero él es inteligente y muy estudioso. Quizás tu hija consiga trabajo primero, pero él conseguirá un trabajo mejor, a su debido tiempo. Así que deja a mi hijo y a los camarones tranquilos.

—Bueno, yo sólo te quería dar un buen consejo. De mi hija no te preocupes, porque seguro que conseguirá un trabajo muy bueno.

82 Todos los caminos llevan a Roma

(all the ways go to Rome)
all roads lead to Rome

—¡Ay, Josefa, estoy tan disgustada con lo de Ramoncito!

—¿Ramoncito? ¿Qué le pasó?

—Todavía no le ha pasado nada. El problema es que ahora dice que quiere ser policía.

—Eso está bien. ¿Qué tiene eso de malo?

—¿Policía? ¡Ay, es peligroso! Y además, yo quería que mi hijo fuera médico y sentirme orgullosa de él.

—Deja que Ramoncito escoja su propia profesión. **Todos los caminos llevan a Roma.**

—¿A Roma? Yo no quiero que vaya a Roma!

—Lo que te quiero decir es que **hay muchas maneras de alcanzar el éxito.** Deja que sea policía si eso es lo que le gusta. Y ya verás cómo tendrá éxito y te sentirás orgullosa de él igual que si fuera médico.

83 Más moscas se cogen con una gota de miel que con un cuarto de vinagre

(more flies are caught with a drop of honey than with a quart of vinegar)

you catch more flies with honey than with vinegar

—Carmen, ¡qué gusto verte! ¿Qué haces por aquí?

—¡Qué sorpresa, Berta! Voy a la floristería a comprar unas flores para mi mamá.

—Ah... ¿es su cumpleaños?

—No, no. Es que ayer tuvimos una pelea tonta, pero quedamos algo enfadadas. Quiero reconciliarme con ella porque es mi mejor amiga.

—Haces muy bien. **Más moscas se cogen con una gota de miel que con un cuarto de vinagre.**

—Sí, es verdad. Estoy convencida de que **da mejores resultados ser amable y cortés con otras personas, mostrarles dulzura y afecto, que tratarlas mal.** Pero es que a veces mi mamá es un poco... digamos difícil.

—Te acompaño en el sentimiento. ¿Qué crees que hago yo aquí?

—¡Vas a comprarle flores a tu mamá también!

84 Matar dos pájaros de un tiro

(to kill two birds with one shot)
to kill two birds with one stone

—¿Cuánto tiempo crees que nos tomará llegar a Barcelona, Maricusa?

—Pues, yo creo que si vamos directo, unas seis horas.

—Estaba pensando que me gustaría visitar a mi tía Adela, que vive en Zaragoza. ¿Crees que podemos hacer esa parada?

—Claro, Ana. Zaragoza está en el camino. Allí podremos descansar un rato y comer algo. Así podemos **matar dos pájaros de un tiro.**

—¿Qué? ¿Qué pájaros vamos a matar?

—Ay, Ana. Quiero decir que podemos **hacer dos cosas al mismo tiempo:** visitar a tu tía y, al mismo tiempo, descansar y comer algo.

—¡Vale!

96

85 Más vale maña que fuerza

(better cunning than force)
better brain than brawn

—Leonardo, yo no me explico cómo pudiste convencer al director que nos dejara hacer esta fiesta. Después de todas las amenazas de protestas que hicimos, parecía imposible.

—No fue fácil, pero lo conseguí. **Más vale maña que fuerza.**

—¿Y cuál fue tu maña? Porque lo que se dice fuerte, no eres, mi amigo.

—Ríete de mí si quieres, pero recuerda quién consiguió el objetivo. Le dije que era mejor tener al estudiantado contento y feliz yendo a muchas fiestas, que triste y deprimido sacando malas calificaciones.

—¿Y esa tontería lo convenció?

—Claro. Si sacamos malas calificaciones y no pasamos de curso, el pobre director no se librará de nosotros jamás. Y eso es algo que el señor director ¡no puede ni imaginarse! ¿Viste como **es mejor resolver los problemas con inteligencia y no con violencia?**

86 Son muchas manos en un plato

(there are too many hands on one plate)
too many cooks spoil the broth

—Mañana Francisca y yo vamos a pintar la casa. ¿Nos quieres ayudar?

—Sí, por supuesto. También tengo tres o cuatro amigos que podrían ayudar.

—Bueno, ya tenemos dos amigos, más tú, Francisca y yo. En total, somos cinco. La casa no es tan grande. Si traemos a más personas **son muchas manos en un plato.**

—Si crees que con cinco personas es suficiente...

—Sí, a veces **cuando son muchas personas tratando de ayudar, las cosas no salen bien.** Es mejor tener menos personas bien organizadas que muchas personas desorganizadas.

—Bueno, pero recuerda que no sólo tenemos manos, sino boca también. ¿Vas a tener refrescos y comida para tus ayudantes?

—Claro que sí. Todos sabemos lo glotón que tú eres. Pero recuerda, si vienes es para ayudar a pintar. No vengas sólo a comer y a tomar refrescos.

Section Seven:
Salud y dinero
Health and Wealth

87 No todo lo que brilla es oro

(not everything that shines is gold)
all that glitters is not gold

—Estoy muy disgustado con el anillo que le compré a mi novia.

—¿Qué pasa? ¿No le gustó el anillo a tu novia?

—No es eso. El problema es que pensé que era de oro de verdad. Se veía muy bonito a la luz del sol. Cuando llegué a la casa, se lo enseñé a mi padre. Él se dio cuenta que no es de oro de verdad, sino de bronce pintado de dorado.

—¡Qué robo! Eso te demuestra que **no todo lo que brilla es oro.**

—Tienes razón, **hay cosas que no son tan valiosas como parecen.**

88 Quien buen vino bebe, despacio envejece

(who drinks good wine, ages slowly)
measure is treasure

—Hoy cumplo cincuenta años, pero me siento como de treinta.

—Claro, con esa forma de vivir que tienes, no vas a envejecer nunca. Nunca peleas, nunca alzas la voz. ¿No tienes sangre o qué?

—Sí tengo sangre y sí me interesa el mundo. Lo que pasa es que **quien buen vino bebe, despacio envejece.**

—¡No me digas!

—Sí te digo... **Hay que saber disfrutar de lo mejor de la vida para mantenerse joven.** Yo me mantengo joven porque sé vivir bien y me rodeo de cosas buenas.

89 Quien quisiere vivir sano, coma poco y cene temprano

(who wants to live healthy, eat little and dine early)
eat breakfast like a king, lunch like a prince, and dinner like a pauper

---

[Dos jóvenes amigos acaban de salir de un restaurante.]

—Oye, Oscar, ¿por qué querías salir a comer tan temprano?

—Es mi costumbre comer temprano.

—No es por nada, pero pareces un viejo comiendo. Comes muy poco, como los viejos. Y los viejos también comen temprano. Y no te gusta salir a las discotecas por la noche. ¿No te parece un poco aburrida tu vida?

—Estás equivocado. **Quien quisiere vivir sano, coma poco y cene temprano.**

—¿Qué me quieres decir, que estoy muy gordo y que me acuesto muy tarde?

—Lo que te digo es que **para tener buena salud es mejor no comer mucho y comer temprano para no acostarse con el estómago lleno.**

—Esos son consejos de viejo.

90 Mente sana en cuerpo sano

(healthy mind in healthy body)
healthy mind, healthy body

—Estoy sorprendido. Ayer vi a mi profesora de filosofía en el gimnasio, haciendo ejercicio.

—¿Por qué te sorprende?

—Es una persona muy intelectual. Pensé que gente como ella utiliza tanto la mente que se olvida que tienen un cuerpo.

—Te equivocas. Yo creo que fue precisamente un filósofo quien dijo: **mente sana en cuerpo sano.**

—Pues parece que ella estudió a ese filósofo, porque sabe que **hay que cuidar el cuerpo al igual que la mente.**

91 La mejor medicina es la buena comida

(the best medicine is good food)
an apple a day keeps the doctor away

—¡Mi padre fue al médico ayer y le mandaron cinco medicinas!

—Es que tu padre no se cuida.

—Nunca se ha alimentado bien. Come mal, con mucha grasa y a cualquier hora. Tiene muchos problemas de estómago, la presión alta, el colesterol alto y principio de diabetes.

—Por eso yo digo que **la mejor medicina es la buena comida.**

—Yo pienso lo mismo. **La persona que sabe alimentarse bien, no tiene necesidad de ir al médico.**

92 No sólo de pan vive el hombre

(not only from bread does man live)
man does not live by bread alone

[Mario se encuentra con Julio en una tienda de música. Mario está sorprendido porque Julio nunca tiene dinero y siempre le pide prestado a los amigos.]

—¡Hola, Julio! Te ves muy contento.

—Sí, me acabo de comprar un disco compacto de mi cantante favorito con el último dinero que me quedaba.

—¿Y eso te pone contento? No es bueno quedarse sin dinero. Es más importante guardar el dinero para comer que gastarlo en discos compactos.

—¡Ay, Mario! No seas tan serio. Recuerda que **no sólo de pan vive el hombre.** ¿Qué sería la vida sin música? A ti también te gusta la música, o no estarías aquí.

—Es cierto. Además, **las necesidades emocionales son tan importantes como las físicas.**

—Ya que estamos de acuerdo, ¿me invitas a almorzar?

93 Más vale pájaro en mano que ciento volando

**(better to have bird in hand
than a hundred flying)**

a bird in the hand is worth two in the bush

—¿Ya vendiste tu carro, Sara?

—Sí, lo vendí muy fácilmente. Alguien vino a ofrecerme un poco menos de lo que yo quería, pero me pagó en efectivo.

—Y tú pensaste que **más vale pájaro en mano que ciento volando.**

—Exactamente. Podría haber esperado a recibir una oferta mejor, pero no tengo paciencia. Además, no sabía si tendría una oferta mejor.

—A veces **es mejor tomar una oferta segura aunque no sea buena, que esperar una oferta mejor pero dudosa.**

—De todos modos, con lo que me pagaron por mi carro viejo, más mis ahorros, ya tengo para comprarme otro carro.

94 Al que madruga Dios lo ayuda

(God helps the one who gets up early)
the early bird catches the worm

—A Julia y a Guillermo les ha ido muy bien con su pequeño negocio.

—Son muy trabajadores. Siempre abren temprano y atraen a muchos clientes. Pronto van a ampliar el negocio.

—Como dice el refrán, **al que madruga Dios lo ayuda.**

—Ellos tienen éxito porque **la gente que trabaja todos los días, se abre camino.**

95 Algo es algo, peor es nada

(something is something, nothing is worse)
better something than nothing

—María, ¿por qué estás tan contenta?

—Tú sabes muy bien que gané una medalla de bronce.

—La medalla que vale es la de oro. Una medalla de bronce no vale nada.

—Mira, **algo es algo, peor es nada.** ¿Acaso tú tienes alguna medalla?

—No yo no tengo ninguna medalla, ni siquiera de aluminio.

—Pues entonces no te burles de mí. Yo estoy contenta porque **es mejor recibir un premio, aunque no sea el primero, a no recibir ninguno.**

96 Vive como rico y ahorrarás como pobre

(live like a rich man and you will save like a poor one)
stretch your arm no further than your sleeve will reach

—Rafael nunca tiene un centavo. Nunca tiene ni para el cine.

—¿Pero cómo va a tener con ese carro tan caro que se compró, y el apartamento de lujo que alquiló?

—Mi madre decía: **Vive como rico y ahorrarás como pobre.**

—Rafael no es responsable con su dinero. **La gente que vive por encima de sus posibilidades nunca puede ahorrar.**

—Y lo peor, un día Rafael puede verse en un serio apuro.

—Cierto. Tendrá que aprender a ahorrar y a no malgastar.

—¡Ojalá que aprenda pronto o lo veo en la calle, sin casa y sin carro!

97 Con dinero baila el perro

(with money the dog dances)
money talks

[Teresa y Felipe han contratado a un payaso para la fiesta de cumpleaños de su niño.]

—Felipe, ¿tú crees que el payaso querrá tirarse a la piscina, después que termine de hacer el espectáculo? Es algo que se me ocurrió ahora, pero no hablamos con él de eso.

—Pues se lo decimos enseguida. Podemos pagarle un poco más. Tú sabes que **con dinero baila el perro.** Y a los niños les va a encantar que lo haga.

—Sí, yo espero que acepte. **Con tal de ganarse un poco de dinero, la gente hace casi cualquier cosa.** Además, sería muy divertido.

98 Come para vivir y no vivas para comer

(eat to live and do not live to eat)
eat to live, not live to eat

[Después de la cena, Cristina se ha servido por tercera vez postre. Su tía la mira y le dice:]

—Cristina, el postre es el final de la cena, no una segunda comida.

—Es que me gusta mucho el dulce, tía. Tú lo sabes.

—Sí, claro que lo sé. Pero mira cómo estás. Te vas a poner como una ballena. **Come para vivir y no vivas para comer.** Te lo he dicho siempre.

—¡Ay, tía! Déjame disfrutar del postre.

—¿Ay, tía? ¿Ay, tía? **No es bueno pasarse el día comiendo,** como tú. ¿No te has mirado en el espejo?

99 Todo sea por el amor al arte

(all be for the love of art)
to be a labor of love

—Buenos días, señora, soy el plomero que le recomendó la Sra. Contreras.

—Buenos días, pase adelante. El trabajo es muy sencillo, hay que romper este baño y poner uno nuevo. Le pagaré lo mismo que le pagó la Sra. Contreras.

—¿Y usted espera que yo haga todo ese trabajo y que **todo sea por el amor al arte?**

—Por amor al arte no. Yo no espero que usted vaya a **hacer el trabajo gratis.** Le dije que le pagaré lo mismo que le pagó la Sra. Contreras.

—Sí, pero el trabajo que yo hice en casa de la Sra. Contreras fue muy sencillo. Era sólo instalar un lavamanos. Aquí hay que hacer el baño completo. Eso cuesta mucho más.

100 Soñar no cuesta nada

(dreaming costs nothing)
it costs nothing to build castles in the air

—Yolanda, ¿ya sabes el último cuento de Nelson?

—Seguro que tiene un cuento nuevo. ¿Qué se le ha ocurrido ahora?

—Ahora dice que se va a Madrid, a torear.

—¿En serio? ¿Pero no dijo la semana pasada que su agente artístico le había conseguido un papel secundario en Hollywood?

—Bueno, lo de Madrid es lo último... En fin, **soñar no cuesta nada.**

—No, no cuesta. Es cierto. **Es fácil vivir de ilusiones.** El despertar, en cambio, no es muy agradable que digamos.

—¡Ahí viene! Vamos a ver qué cuento tiene ahora.

101 Borrón y cuenta nueva

(smudge and new account)
clean slate

[Diego llama a Javier por teléfono.]

—¿Javier? ¿Cómo estás? Soy Diego.

—Yo bien, ¿y tú?

—Regular. Tengo un problema grande. Quiero ir a una fiesta con Silvia, pero el carro no me funciona.

—No te preocupes, Diego, yo te presto el mío. Tiene el tanque lleno de gasolina y todo. Así que no te tienes que preocupar de nada. Ahora mismo voy para allá para llevarte el carro.

—¡Oye, tú sí que eres buen amigo! Mira, el dinero que te presté la semana pasada, no te preocupes de devolvérmelo. **Borrón y cuenta nueva.**

—¿En serio?

—Sí, no te preocupes de pagar la deuda; **estamos parejos.**

Translations
Traducciones

---

1 (page 3)

"Manuel, I have a secret to tell you."

"What is it about, Isabel?"

"It's something they told me about you."

"Tell me right now."

"No. Not right now. Here at the office is not a good place. You know, **walls have ears.** People in this office are always gossiping. It's best if we meet in the park, after work."

"Right. Here at the office, **someone can hear us without us noticing.**"

"Okay, so I'll wait for you in the park and I'll tell you everything."

---

2 (page 4)

"Your father seems to be a rigid, demanding man."

"Not really. He is just the opposite. My father is loving, understanding, and kind. He gives you that impression because he has faced many hard times in life. You only know him from the outside. I know him inside."

"I understand. Like my grandmother says: **Cold hands, warm heart.**"

"Precisely. **Some people may seem harsh on the outside but they are good inside.**"

---

3 (page 5)

"Carmen, my mother-in-law is very angry with me."

"What happened?"

"I simply recommended a very good diet program to her, because she's very overweight."

"Who asked you to do that? It's best not to say anything. You know that **a closed mouth catches no flies.**"

"I only wanted to give her some good advice."

"Remember that **it's best to be silent because talking can get you into trouble.**"

"You are absolutely right! I'll have to be more careful about what I say to her."

---

4 (page 6)

"Hello, Carlos! How's it going with your new computer?"

"Well, it's nothing out of this world."

"Wasn't it a birthday gift from your parents?"

"Yes, but it's a small laptop good enough to do course-related work at the university and get on the Internet. But the screen is not in color and it doesn't have any of the computer games I like."

"But, Carlos! What are you complaining about? **Don't look a gift horse in the mouth.** I wish my parents would give me a present like the computer you got."

"You're right. **It's not fair to complain about a present that was given to me.**"

5 (page 7)

[Esperanza and her husband are attending a very elegant reception, honoring a visiting diplomat.]

"Rebeca looks so elegant today!" says Esperanza. "I have never seen her wearing such an expensive dress."

"She may be wearing a very expensive dress, but her bad manners have not changed."

"You can tell her bad taste by the way she talks. Right now she's talking with her mouth full. That goes to show you that **you can't make a silk purse out of a sow's ear.**"

"Unfortunately, **a person cannot hide her lack of education or bad manners even if she wears expensive clothes.**"

---

6 (page 8)

"This is a big investment, Alina. Have you considered all the risks involved?"

"Yes," answers Alina, not very convinced.

"From the way you answer, I don't believe you. Look, before doing anything, **it's better to sleep on it.**"

"Sleep on it?"

"Yes. **Wait until tomorrow to make a decision.** That way, you'll have more time to think about the matter."

"Right. It's best to wait another day before I sign any papers and deliver a check. I'll think it through and through."

---

7 (page 9)

[A young man is at the movies. The film has not started yet. He takes a seat and places a magazine on it to reserve it. Then he goes to get a soda. When he comes back, a man has taken his seat.]

"Excuse me, sir, but that's my seat."

"It's yours, young man? You brought it from home?"

"No, I didn't bring it from home, but I was already sitting there. I went to get a soda and left a magazine on it to reserve it."

"I'm sorry, young man. **Possession is nine-tenths of the law.** Your magazine is now on the seat behind me."

"But, what gives you the right?"

"Look, young man. You left your seat. **If you leave your place, when you come back, you can expect someone else to have taken it.** It's your fault, not mine."

---

8 (page 10)

"You know, this new priest we have at the church has some very modern ideas."

"What ideas does he have?"

"I was complaining about the bad luck I've had in my life. I've never had a good job. My wife left me because of my drinking. My children don't want to visit me. I thought it was the devil's work, but the priest told me: **every man is the architect of his own fortune.**"

"I agree with him. **Each person is responsible for his life and for improving it with his own effort.**"

---

9 (page 11)

"I can't find my little phone book. Have you seen it? Where could I have put it?".

"How could you know? Look how messy your room is!"

"It's a little book with a blue cover. You must have seen it."

"I haven't seen anything. If you had **a place for everything and everything in its place,** you would have already found it."

"Yes, Mom, I know, **it's important to be organized.** You've told me many times, but right now I'm in a hurry and I need my little book."

"So, if you know you should be more organized, why aren't you? Here's your little book. It was in the kitchen. You have so much room next to the phone, and yet you leave it in the kitchen. I don't know how much longer you're going to be this way."

---

10 (page 12)

"Carlos, I told you a long time ago to take the garbage out."

"Are you sure, Mom? I didn't hear you."

"There's none..."

"Yes, I know... **There's none so deaf as those who will not hear.** You tell me the same thing every day."

"It's just that **you only hear what's convenient for you.** I'm tired of telling you things and not have you pay attention to me."

---

11 (page 13)

"Rafael, have you seen Rosa's new boyfriend?"

"Yes, it's a guy much older than she is."

"The truth is that I can't understand why Rosa has such a boyfriend. She's so young, pretty, and intelligent. She deserves someone as young as she is."

"Oh, Alberto! **Let sleeping dogs lie.**"

"Why do you say that?"

"You have your own girlfriend and you were never interested in Rosa. Let Rosa decide about her own life. **Don't meddle in matters that don't concern you.**"

---

12 (page 14)

"Did you see the interview last night on TV with Miss Universe?"

"That reporter was very bad. He told Miss Universe that he couldn't understand why she had won the contest."

"And Miss Universe gave him a very good answer. She told him that it was natural that he couldn't understand because only intelligent people can appreciate her beauty and talent."

"She gave him a very good answer. **A word once spoken is past recalling.**"

"Miss Universe showed him that **a person should think before he speaks.**"

13 (page 15)

"Rigoberto, I saw you smoking this afternoon. As your father, I have the obligation to give you some advice. Smoking is bad for your health. You're very young. It would be best if you stopped smoking."

"You? Telling me to stop smoking? I learned it from you. In all my 19 years I've always seen you smoking. You live by the old saying, **do as I say, not as I do,** right?"

"You're right, **it's not right to deny others something you're not willing to give up yourself.** But the truth is that I've been smoking for many years and it's hard to quit. I wish my father had talked me into not smoking when I was your age."

14 (page 16)

"Hello, Lalo. How're you doing, man? What are you up to?"

"I'm fine, Rodolfo, just very busy. I got a job."

"Work? I can't believe it! And how long is that new illness going to last?"

"It's not an illness. I like this job and I want to keep it. You should do the same, man."

"What are you trying to say? That **work helps you stay out of trouble,** like the old saying goes?"

"Right, Rodolfo. Before, you and I would hang out, play pool, watch TV, just wasting time. **Working is a way of spending time in something productive and avoiding bad habits.**"

"You've become really boring. Stop giving me advice."

15 (page 17)

"Come on, guys, run! We have to go before the owners of the house come out."

"I don't think we should leave, Jaime. We should tell them we did it."

"Are you crazy, Miguel? They would certainly call the police and our parents. I don't want to get into any kind of trouble!"

"Don't be cowards, guys. **What's done is done.**"

"Listen Miguel. It's true that **we should take responsibility for our actions and face the consequences.** But don't call us cowards because that offends me. I'll accept being called bad pitchers and even worse batters."

"Gee, Luis! Why did you forget to mention horrible fielders?"

16 (page 18)

"Mirta, is it true that you're leaving your job and going to work for a small company?"

"Yes, I already made up my mind. I'm leaving next month."

"Do you think that's a good idea? Isn't it better to work for a large company, with more prestige and greater opportunities?"

"It depends on how you look at it. At the large company I'll never have an important job. I've been in the same position for three years. But at the smaller company, they've offered me a managerial position."

"I see, you figured that it's **better to be the head of a dog than the tail of a lion.**"

"That's right. For me, **it's better to be a leader in something small than to be the last one in something big.**"

"Well, good luck with your new job!"

---

17 (page 21)

"Fernando, what do you think of our new swimming coach? He seems a bit old. I'd like a younger coach."

"I thought the same thing the first time I saw him. But I've come to realize that he has a lot of experience and he knows what he's doing."

"But don't you think it would be better to have a young coach?"

"Not necessarily. Remember that **the devil knows many things because he's old.**"

"That's right. He was a championship swimmer when he was young. He's been teaching for many years. **His age is an advantage because it means more experience.**"

"Exactly. A young coach wouldn't be as good as he is."

---

18 (page 22)

"Margarita, I don't know what to do with my son. On Sundays, he spends the whole day watching sports on TV. He's 17 now. It would be better for him to spend his time studying or working."

"I don't think he's to blame. His father does the same thing. **Like father, like son.**"

"Yes, **my son has the same bad habits that his father has.**"

"The best thing is to talk to him so that he realizes that he's wasting too much time watching TV. At his age, he needs to use his time well, studying or working."

---

19 (page 23)

[Sonia is a university professor who has just come home. Her husband, Vicente, and her two children are waiting for her.]

"How did the afternoon go? Did the children do their homework?"

"They had little homework to do. They finished right away and I let them play with your computer."

"Play with my computer?"

"And the news isn't very good. It looks like they erased several documents."

"Why didn't you give them more homework or sit down to study with them? You know that **the devil finds work for idle hands to do.**"

"You're right. I shouldn't have left them alone with your computer. **When children have nothing to do, they get into mischief.**"

---

20 (page 24)

"Yesterday I had a very unpleasant experience at the restaurant. The waiter took a long time to wait on me. It was an elegant restaurant and I didn't want to call his name out."

"And where was your waiter that he didn't take care of you?"

"There was another table with a very bad-mannered lady. She wasn't at all shy about yelling out and waving her arms to get his attention."

"You know that **the squeaky wheel gets the oil.**"

"I believe you should show good manners at a restaurant. I would feel bad raising my voice. But it's true that **those who complain get better service.**"

---

21 (page 25)

"Where are you going all dressed up, Jaime?"

"I'm going to my grandmother's graduation."

"Your grandmother's graduation? I don't get it."

"She just finished her studies at the university. She says that as a young woman she never had the money or the time to study and that **you're never too old to learn.**"

"What did your grandmother study?"

"She studied history. She thought that with all the years she's lived, studying history would be easy."

"That's wonderful! That goes to show you that **studying is not just for young people, but for any age.** Congratulate your grandmother for me."

"Thanks, Mirta! Well, I have to go, or I'm going to be the one who's late."

---

22 (page 26)

"Julito is a very good kid."

"His grandparents raised him very well. He is studious, respectful, and hard working."

"Yes. Luckily, he was raised by his grandparents. We all know that his mother and father are kind of crazy and disorganized."

"Thanks to his grandparents he has very good qualities. And now that he's going on to college, do you think he will change?"

"Absolutely not. I don't think so. **What's learned in the cradle lasts 'til the tomb.**"

"You're right. **The habits that you pick up as a child stay with you your whole life.**"

---

23 (page 27)

"How did the trip go? Did you have a good time?"

"Oh, dear, our daughter really embarrassed me at the airport."

"Laurita? Why? What did she do?"

"Just imagine, before taking off, while waiting at the gate, all the seats were taken. And do you know what your daughter did? She walked up to one of the men who was sitting and said to him: 'Can't you see that my mom is pregnant? Would you please give her your seat?'"

"Oh, that's my daughter for you! She did the right thing. She spoke the truth. You know that **out of the mouths of babes ....**"

"I was very embarrassed. People surely thought that I had told her to find a seat for me."

"Don't worry, people know that **children are very sincere and that they say what they feel.**"

24 (page 28)

"I've decided to have some plastic surgery. I'm 55 years old now and I don't like to look old. My wife is 20 years younger than me. I don't want people to think that she's my daughter. You know that **you can't turn back the clock.**"

"Don't be silly. It's good that you take care of your appearance, but plastic surgery is very expensive."

"It's just that I don't want to look old."

"**It's not good to hide your age.** It's better to face up to how old you are."

25 (page 29)

"My father warned me not to buy a motorcycle. He said they are dangerous and not very practical."

"And what did you do?"

"Well, I bought a motorcycle anyway because I really wanted one."

"What did your father say when he found out?"

"Not much. He looked at me with a stern face, shook his head and said: **'Advice when most needed is least heeded.'**"

"He's right. **Advice from older people helps us get the protection we need in life.** There are many motorcycle accidents. If I were you, I would sell it and get myself a car, like your father says."

26 (page 30)

"Oh, Gladys! My son is driving me crazy!"

"What's wrong? Is he misbehaving?"

"The problem is that he likes to take toys away from his brothers, but he won't share his. If anyone touches his toys he throws a tantrum. I don't want to have a selfish son like that."

"Well, then try to teach him to share. You know that's hard; **as the twig is bent, so is the tree inclined.**"

"You'll see; I'll teach him. They say that **everyone is destined to be a certain way from the time they are born and nothing will change them.** But I'll change my son."

27 (page 33)

"What are you thinking about, Sergio?"

"I've got some money saved and I want to invest it in some business. I was thinking of buying shares at a computer company."

"Be careful. Remember that the economy is not in good shape. Haven't you read the paper?"

"Yes, I have. But I have also read that some computer companies are doing very well."

"Think about what you do with your money. Remember that **forewarned is forearmed.**"

"You're right. I already have the information. I know exactly which are the good companies and which are the bad ones. **It's a great advantage to proceed with care** in business."

28 (page 34)

"I'm furious! I just got back from the supermarket. The owner had me stopped on the way out and had someone check my bag. How disrespectful! It's the second time they've treated me as if I were some kind of thief."

"That's insulting. They did the same thing to me last week. The owner is very distrusting."

"That's because he's not an honest person. He charges really high prices. He's the one who's stealing from all of us. And you know that **there's no honor among thieves.**"

"That's why the owner treats his customers badly. **A dishonest person thinks that everyone is dishonest.**"

"Well, he made a big mistake with me. I will never again shop at that super-market."

29 (page 35)

"We have to give some good advice to our friend Isabel."

"What's her problem?"

"She's looking for a boyfriend. And she says she wants a boyfriend with a career and money, who only wears a suit and tie."

"I see. Isabel should know that **clothes do not make the man.**"

"Of course not. Many professional people do not dress with a suit and tie. **You can't judge them from the way they dress.** You have to know people to know what they are like."

"And there are also men who spend what little money they make on good clothes, even though they don't earn much and are not professionals."

30 (page 36)

"Did you see what happened to Nelson?"

"Yes, he got a ticket for speeding on the highway."

"Do you remember how he always made fun of my driving? He said I drove too slowly and took too many precautions. He would see me at the wheel and start laughing."

"Well, look at him now. You can feel satisfied. **He who laughs last, laughs best.**"

"I'm glad he got a ticket. That way he will learn not to speed. **Although he used to laugh at me, he will now realize that he was wrong and that I was right.**"

31 (page 37)

[Efraín is convinced that there is life on the moon.]

"Ester, I saw a show on TV yesterday about life on the moon."

"That's not possible, Efraín. There's no life on the moon."

"Well, I saw it with my own eyes."

"Don't you know that there isn't even oxygen on the moon? Water and oxygen are necessary for life."

"Well, I don't know if there is or there isn't any oxygen, but I did see those who live on the moon."

"I see that you really know nothing. **He that knows nothing, doubts nothing.**"

"Why do you say that?"

"Because **people who are not informed can believe anything.** Did you also know that the world is flat?"

---

32 (page 38)

"Ana María, what did you think of Carlos?"

"He seems very nice, but not very smart."

"Why do you say that?"

"Virginia has a class with him. She tells me that Carlos is always studying, but he gets very bad grades. And you know what they say: **send a donkey to Paris, and he will return no wiser than he went.**"

"Poor Carlos! I don't like it when they make fun of him. It's true that **he's not very smart, since he studies a lot and doesn't learn much.** But he is a good, funny, and happy person."

---

33 (page 39)

"Berta, last night a man knocked on my door. I looked through the window and I thought he looked like my brother-in-law Armando. You know, **all cats are gray in the dark.**"

"Yes, it's true that **everyone looks the same in the dark.** And what happened—was it Armando?"

"No way! When I turned on the porch light to open the door, I saw that it was some stranger. Good thing I didn't open the door. We peered at each other through the door window, and he had a surprised look on his face. He stepped back, looking over the house and the address. Then he apologized profusely for bothering me, and he walked away."

"Don't tell me he had the wrong house."

"You got it. It seems that in the dark, all houses look the same too, huh?"

---

34 (page 40)

[Patricia and Ramón talk about the new man who has come to work at the company.]

"Have you noticed how much the new guy talks?" asks Patricia.

"Yes. He is always judging everything. He knows everything and he is never in agreement with anyone," says Ramón.

"And he talks nonstop."

"Nonstop. As my wife always says: **empty vessels make the most noise.**"

"We have the perfect example here. I think the new guy is trying to make a good impression."

"But his behavior has the opposite effect. **When someone talks as much as he does, it's because he's trying to hide his own ignorance.**"

"Careful! Here he comes. Well, I'm going back to my desk so that I don't have to hear him talk."

35 (page 41)

"That TV show doesn't convince me. The man claims to be a psychic who has studied the stars and knows a lot about astrology and what have you. But I don't think he knows much of anything."

"You're right, **the greatest scholars are not the best preachers.**"

"I prefer to watch programs with psychologists or sociologists who explain how people behave and why. **People who really know something share what they know without making so much noise.**"

36 (page 42)

[Two neighbors are having a conversation through their porch windows.]

"María, you know that Laura loves to say mean things about you. The other day I had to tell her: 'Look, Laura, María is my neighbor. She is a very nice person and I don't want you to talk about her.'"

"Thank you, but you know what? **What the eye doesn't see, the heart doesn't grieve over.**"

"Certainly, of course, but I just wanted you to know that she's the one who's saying nasty things about you."

"Thank you, but I would rather not know anything about that. **What you don't see with your own eyes or hear with your own ears can't hurt you.** Thank you for your concern, but I have more important things to do besides worrying about trying to be everyone's friend."

37 (page 43)

"Tell me, Lidia, how's your brother? You haven't talked about him for a while."

"He's fine, as always. He still doesn't have a job. He says he wants to be a painter and spends all day in his room oil painting. I'm tired of the smell of the paint."

"Do you think he's a good painter?"

"Well, I have to **give credit where credit is due.** My brother may have his faults, but he is a good painter. He does wonderful paintings. I think he will be successful some day."

"**It's good that you can recognize someone else's talent!** And what about you, are you a talented painter, too?"

"Me? Not at all! I'm not anything like my brother. I'm going to be a scientist!"

38 (page 44)

[Two friends are talking in the school yard during recess.]

"Did you hear Pedro?"

"Yes, there he goes again."

"He says he's going to study languages, computers, and then medicine."

"He's going to be like my uncle says: **jack of all trades, master of none.**"

"Certainly. He's going to be an amateur in all three things. At the end, he won't know any language well and he won't master computers."

"And as for me, I would never be crazy enough to see him as a doctor, not even for a corn on my toe."

"Me neither. **People who want to learn too many things at the same time end up learning none well.**"

---

39 (page 45)

"Marina, how did the trial go today?"

"Fabulously well. Fortunately, I had photos of the accident to show the judge that my client was innocent."

"And what did the other lawyer do?"

"He had a lot of papers. But you know that **a picture is worth a thousand words.** I won the case."

"So, it's true that **a good photograph can be the best explanation.**"

---

40 (page 46)

"Santiago, I have to confess something to you."

"Tell me, Irene, why do you look so serious, honey?"

"It's just that I'm not in love with you."

"What? Are you joking?"

"I'm not joking. **Honesty is the best policy.** You're very nice, but I'm not in love with you."

"Why didn't you tell me before?"

"I didn't want to hurt your feelings, but my mother advised me that **it's better to tell the truth, even if it hurts, than to lie.**"

---

41 (page 47)

"Paco, you have just finished your French course and now you tell me you want to start studying Japanese. Don't you get tired of studying so much?"

"No, Micaela. I love to study."

"But, why do you study languages? You're afraid of airplanes! You'll never visit the countries where those languages are spoken. Really, Paco, I don't understand."

"It doesn't matter. **Knowledge is power.** Even if I never go to those countries, maybe I'll find a job where they need someone who can speak different languages. **It's always good to know more.** You never know when all that knowledge can come in handy."

---

42 (page 48)

"José just got disqualified from tomorrow's raise because he forgot to fill out the forms. That's quite a silly mistake he made!"

"I can't believe he forgot. I reminded him several times. He always said he would take care of it."

"Well, he didn't. And now he tells me that it's not his fault, that he didn't know he had to fill out a form."

"Of course, **no fool thinks he's a fool.**"

"True. **Nobody likes to admit his own lack of intelligence.**"

43 (page 51)

"The contract is only for two years and it doesn't offer many advantages."

"Yes, I know. But you'll have to live all that time in another country, in a culture different from yours. That's like getting married. My mother says: **'look before you leap.'**"

"You're right. I'm going to give it some more thought."

"Before making an important decision, think about what you're doing. Take your time. Don't just look at the earnings, look at your losses, too."

"Right. If I take that job, I'll be away from my parents and my friends... I'll give it some more thought. I have a whole month to decide. Thanks for the warning."

44 (page 52)

"We haven't gotten a raise here for a while. If we want a raise, we'll have to join forces."

"Do you think the owner will listen to us?"

"Of course he will! **In unity there's strength.** All of us workers have to get together. We know that if we stay divided we won't gain anything, but **if we unite, we will succeed.**"

"Good idea. Let's have a meeting this afternoon, after work. All the workers need to be there. We have to make a petition together. It's the only way to improve things."

45 (page 53)

"Why did you give money to that man on the street? Don't you know that he's a good-for-nothing vagrant?"

"Well, he seemed very poor and he asked me for money. What was I supposed to do? I always think: **a good deed is never lost.**"

"But it's not a good thing to give money to someone who doesn't work and spends the whole time begging."

"I try not to judge anyone. I think that **if someone is in need, one should try to help him without imposing any conditions.**"

"I don't know if you've really done a good deed or a bad one."

46 (page 54)

"Our neighbor is very odd. He doesn't speak much and spends the whole day at home reading."

"You've never spoken to him?"

"No. He seems to work at night, but we don't know what he does."

"Well, **know your neighbor from the books he reads.**"

"You've said it. **The books a person reads are a good way of knowing his values and what he's like.** And you know what? I think our neighbor is a murderer! He's always reading police novels!"

"Don't be silly! My brother knows your neighbor. He's not a murderer. He's a police officer who works the night shift!"

47 (page 55)

"Joaquín, I heard the good news that Ileana and you are getting married."

"Yes, next month it will be a year since we met. We're getting married on that date, exactly a year after we met."

"Will the wedding be on a Saturday?"

"No, it's a Tuesday. We want to marry then because it's a very important date for us."

"Listen, that's not a good idea. Wise men say **never marry or take a trip on Tuesday.**"

"That's an old superstition and I don't believe it. It's not true that **it's bad luck to marry or to take a trip on Tuesday.** I won't listen to you. Ileana and I will get married on that day, whatever people say. Our mind is made up. That very day, we'll start our honeymoon on a Caribbean cruise. I know we'll be very happy."

48 (page 56)

"Do you know that Carmen and Julio are getting married?"

"They've been dating for two years, right?"

"Yes, but they are both very selfish and disorganized. Julio never has a steady job and he is always going out with his friends instead of taking Carmen out. And Carmen, instead of talking about it with him, is always in conflict with his friends. But they say they're very much in love and that they want to get married."

"Julio is not the ideal husband, nor is Carmen the ideal wife. Truly, **love is blind!**"

"Yes, it seems like **they love each other so much, they don't see each other's faults.**"

"Well, my friend, if you ever see me in the same situation, ready to marry someone who's not right for me, please tell me. I don't want to make the same mistake Carmen is making."

"I promise I will."

49 (page 57)

"Julia is the best supervisor I've had in my whole life. That's the truth."

"You're right. She's always on the lookout for any problem we may have and she'll even ask us about our families. She is exceptional."

"That's why so many people love her here at the company."

"It's just that **one good turn deserves another.** That's the way it is."

"It's like a law of the universe, like the law of gravity, or one of those laws of physics. This one is the law of love. **If you give love, you will receive love.** It's always true."

50 (page 58)

"Rogelio, I'd like to invite you to the football game on Sunday. I have two tickets."

"No, thank you. I prefer to spend Sundays with my friend the mechanic. That way I help him and get to learn, too. You know I love mechanics."

"I think it's more fun to go to a football game, but, anyway, **birds of a feather flock together.**"

"Invite Néstor. He really loves football. He'll go with you. **People with the same tastes or interests always look for a way to get together.**"

---

51 (page 59)

[Adela is complaining about her husband to her friend Lola. Her friend replies:]

"I'm surprised to hear you talk that way. Didn't you always say that Pablito was the most loving, intelligent, and capable man on the planet? Where have all your praises gone?"

"You can imagine," says Adela sadly, **"familiarity breeds contempt."**

"You see? **Over the years, we come to recognize others' faults.** It's the same thing with husbands. The wedding and the first few years are like a dream, but then, reality sets in. Why is it that when we get married we think that everything will always be like the honeymoon?"

"I don't know. But the truth is that it was a mistake to marry my husband. We're no longer happy."

---

52 (page 60)

"Rogelio, I don't like those new friends of yours. Where did you find them? What do they do?"

"Don't worry, Dad. I know who my friends are."

"Be careful, son, remember that **if you lie down with dogs, you'll get up with fleas.**"

"I know, you've told me many times."

"I'll never get tired of telling you. **People influence each other.** I don't want you to get into any trouble."

"I know, I know. The truth is that I've only known them for a short time, but don't worry. I'll be on the lookout. Do you trust your son or not?"

---

53 (page 61)

"We've been living in this house for twenty years. The neighbors next door have also lived in their house twenty years."

"Are you good friends?"

"We're more than friends. You know that **good neighbors are hard to find.** We are like family. We visit each other and we help each other out when there's a need."

"You lucked out; not everyone has good neighbors. **Having a good neighbor is like having family next door.**"

---

54 (page 62)

"Omar, did you know you're earning a reputation as someone who cheats and lies?"

"Me? Why?"

"Because your best friend, Rubén, was cheating on the history test. Everyone thought he was a good student, but he turned out to be a cheat."

"But I am a good student."

"People said the same thing about Rubén before. And since the two of you are

130

always together... You know what people think: **a man is known by the company he keeps.**"

"Yes, I know that **people think that you are the same as your friends.**"

"Well, if you want to protect your reputation as a good student, don't be so close to a cheat like Rubén. Find your friends among other honest students like you."

---

55 (page 63)

"Carlos, they tell me that you are always in the company of Alberto and Matías. Is that true?"

"And... why do you ask?"

"Everyone knows that they are always getting into trouble. I don't think it's a good idea for you to be friends with them."

"Jorge, you are my older brother, but that doesn't give you the right to choose my friends. Besides, people don't say very nice things about you either, in case you didn't know."

"Oh, Carlitos, haven't you ever heard that you should **select your friends with a silk-gloved hand?**"

"Those are things old people love to say, Jorge. What does it mean, anyway?"

"It means that **you can't choose your family, but you can choose your friends.** In fact, do you know why people say nasty things about me? Because a long time ago I was friends with the wrong crowd, and people have not yet forgotten."

---

56 (page 64)

"Nancy, did you switch hairdressers yet?"

"Not yet. I'm still with the same one who burned my hair last time I tried to get a permanent."

"How is that possible? You told me that after what he had done to your hair, you hated him and would never go back to him."

"Yes, that's what I said, Violeta. But my hairdresser promised to do my hair for free two more times to make up for his mistake. I've been going to him for a long time. He already knows my taste and doesn't charge me much. I thought, well, **better the devil you know than the devil you don't know.** So, I forgave him."

"I understand, sometimes **it's best to keep what you have, even if it's not perfect, than to run the risk of changing for something better and come out losing.**"

---

57 (page 67)

"What a pity! They don't have chocolate ice cream."

"Why don't you order another flavor?"

"Chocolate is the only ice cream flavor I like. It doesn't matter. Now that I think about it, it's better that way. **Every cloud has a silver lining.**"

"Why do you say that?"

"It's just that I'm too fat. If I keep on eating so much chocolate ice cream, I'm going to get even fatter. **Sometimes, what seems to be a problem is in fact a help.**"

"Yes, it's best to keep a positive attitude and to see the good side of everything."

58 (page 68)

"We are getting a group together to go on a boat tour this Sunday. Do you want to come?"

"Me? Never! I already went on a boat tour last year and I almost died."

"What happened?"

"The boat had some engine trouble. We were stranded in the middle of the ocean. We had to call for rescue on the radio."

"But the boat we are taking on Sunday is new and the engine is excellent."

"No, thank you. You know that **once bitten twice shy.**"

"I understand. **If you've had a big scare, the fear stays with you.**"

59 (page 69)

"Have you found a job yet, Pedro?"

"Nothing at all. They offered me a job, but it was too far from home and I don't have a car."

"Can't you take the bus?"

"The problem is that the bus takes too long. I would have to leave home at 6 in the morning to get to work at 8. I still haven't answered them to let them know if I'm taking the job or not."

"That's no problem at all. **Don't make a mountain out of a molehill.** You can take the bus to work. And in two or three months you can buy a car with your earnings."

"In reality, **my problem is not so bad.** I need a job. I'll tell them I'll take it and later on I'll buy a car."

60 (page 70)

"What I like most about my boss is that he's always arguing and scolding us."

"And you like that?"

"Yes, this boss we have now yells and screams when I come in late or if he doesn't like something, but he doesn't do anything. You know that **barking dogs seldom bite.**"

"I see what you mean. The boss we had before him never scolded us or yelled at us, but he was treacherous. On payday, he would deduct money from your pay for coming in late."

"That's what I mean. This new boss is **someone who screams and threatens, but does no harm.**"

"Even so, it's better not to push it. It's true that he doesn't bite, but stop coming in late so he'll stop barking. All that barking from the boss is not pleasant."

61 (page 71)

"It has really rained hard, Emilio!"

"Don't remind me. My basement's flooded. Now I'll have to clean it up and remove the carpeting. It's a lot of work."

"We didn't have any problems at my house. I'll help you out."

"Don't worry. I don't want to bother you."

"It's no bother. That's what friends are for, right?"

132

"I would really appreciate it. **A friend in need is a friend indeed.**"

"I will be very glad to help you. **True friends help each other in time of need.**"

---

62 (page 72)

"Rodolfo, is it true that you want to leave your job?"

"Yes, Raúl. My sister gave me a job at her company. But the truth is that I don't like it as much as I thought. And I've received another job offer, but I don't want to leave my sister out in the cold. She needs a worker."

"Listen, Rodolfo. I don't have a job. What if you tell your sister about me? I'll take your place and that way you won't disappoint her and I'll have a job."

"That's not a bad idea, Raúl. They say that **one man's gravy is another man's poison.**"

"You can see, Rodolfo, that **what's bad or uncomfortable for one person may turn out to be good and comfortable for someone else.**"

"You're going to like my job, Raúl. Besides, my sister is very nice to everyone, except her own brother."

---

63 (page 73)

"Sit down. I have bad news for you."

"What's wrong? Judging from your face, it looks like the world is coming to an end."

"I just lost my job."

"Well, is that all? That's not the end of the world."

"Isn't that bad enough for you? I don't have a job anymore."

"Ricardo, **keep your chin up.** You won't gain anything by getting depressed and torturing yourself. **The best thing is to face problems with a positive attitude.** That's all you have to do. So, cheer up and smile. I'll take you to the movies. You'll have time to look for a job tomorrow."

---

64 (page 74)

"You can see where debts have taken me: I've lost my car, my house on the beach, my credit. In fact, I'm destroyed."

"Maybe hit, but not beaten. You simply have to learn your lesson and start anew. **When one door shuts, another opens.**"

"Oh, I'm in no mood for old sayings!"

"It's not a saying, it's the truth. I've gone through the same thing. **Behind a big problem there's always some help or something better.** That's why I'm telling you, take this opportunity to organize your finances. Get on the right path. You'll see how you'll get your life back together."

---

65 (page 75)

[Tatiana is talking on the phone with her friend Marta.]

"We're not going to the beach. José doesn't want to go. Or he pretends that he doesn't. I don't know."

"In that case, come yourself, with your son."

"No. He says we shouldn't go. He says that if he wants to stay home, it's not right for us to leave him all alone on a Sunday."

"Oh, your husband proves that **misery loves company.**"

"That's his big mistake. He's always been that way. **He neither does what he wants, nor does he let others do what they want.**"

"But those times are gone, my dear friend. Please!"

"That's true. Wait for me, I'm coming over with my son. I think that today is a good day to teach a lesson to this husband of mine."

---

66 (page 76)

[Elena calls her husband, Alejandro, at work to tell him that their daughter Luisita has just failed another subject.]

"Why are you calling me at work with such urgency?"

"Isn't that enough reason for you? This is the second subject that Luisita has failed. This daughter of yours is going to kill me. She'll never amount to anything in life."

"She's not my daughter alone. She's your daughter, too. And, really, it's not such a big deal. **Nothing is certain but death and taxes.** Let's find a tutor who can help her do her homework. That will show her how to study better and get better grades. **The problem is not so bad.**"

"Let's hope that will solve it."

---

67 (page 77)

[The grandmother is talking to her oldest granddaughter. The granddaughter wants to get even with a friend for speaking badly of her.]

"I don't think you should want to seek vengeance on your friend. What will you gain?"

"What will I gain? Nothing short of revenge for everything she has done to me. Isn't that enough? She will pay for it, one way or another. Now it's my turn to speak badly of Susana and spread rumors about her."

"Oh, my sweetie, that's not right. **You reap what you sow.** Learn to forgive. What's done is done. **If you do someone wrong, or if you foster hate, it will all come back to you.**"

"I don't believe so. Anyway, I'm not interested. What I want is revenge from Susana for speaking badly of me."

"Think about what you're doing. I've done my duty by giving you my advice."

---

68 (page 78)

"Yesterday, when I went out, I took my umbrella with me, but it didn't rain. Today, I'm going to leave the umbrella behind. It's cumbersome to carry around all the time. Besides, I'll be worried about losing it."

"Listen, be glad it didn't rain yesterday. But I think that it will rain today. You should take the umbrella with you. Remember: **better safe than sorry.**"

"Yes, **it's preferable to put up with a small inconvenience rather than face a bigger one.** Taking an umbrella everywhere is no fun, but getting wet is even worse."

"The same thing happens to me all the time. Whenever I take my umbrella with me, it doesn't rain. But every time I leave it at home, it does."

134

"Okay, I'll take the umbrella with me. And if I lose it, I can always blame it on you."

---

69 (page 79)

"Liliana, is it true that the university president has resigned?"

"Yes, unfortunately it's true. It's already been three weeks and they haven't found anyone to replace her."

"They tell me that things over there are a mess; you know that **the woman is the key of the house.**"

"Exactly. Since she resigned, the university is in **a state of total chaos because it has no direction.**"

"It's too bad. She was an excellent president. And where is she working now?"

"Well... She went to climb Mt. Everest! She said that she was tired of so much work and organization."

"Wow!"

---

70 (page 80)

"Carla, I'm very upset with you. Who worked harder to raise the funds for the new library? Was it you or me?"

"Well... of course... you did, Tina."

"Then why does your name appear in this article as the main person?"

"The journalist must have... made a mistake! That's it, that's what happened. I gave him your name and mine. I swear."

"This is incredible. **You should not reap the benefits of someone else's labor.** I spent the whole year working, but **you took advantage of all my efforts.**"

"I'm sorry, Tina."

"I'm more sorry than you are, Carla. You've just lost a friend."

---

71 (page 81)

"Did you like the movie?"

"It has a good plot. And Regina is my favorite actress. But I believe that in some scenes her acting was not very good."

"She's a very good actress, but **nobody's perfect.**"

"Since she's my favorite actress, I'm a little demanding with her. I know that **nobody is perfect,** but I have this illusion that she is. That's why I hate to see her acting poorly."

"Well, since you know so much about acting, write her a letter with your good advice."

---

72 (page 82)

"Mom, do you have anything for a stomachache? I feel really bad."

"I warned you not to eat so much pizza. **After the feast comes the reckoning.** So, don't complain now."

"You're right. **I enjoyed it too much and now I'm paying the consequences.**"

"Well, I'll bring you some water with baking soda. You'll feel better soon."

73 (page 85)

"You're finally here, Miguel! We were all worried."

"Excuse me for being so late for lunch. I don't know the area and I got lost on the way here. I couldn't find the restaurant."

"Don't worry. **Better late than never.**"

"Thank you, Marta. I also thought that it would be **better to arrive late than not arrive at all.**"

"We already ordered, but, as you can see, we haven't started eating yet. We delayed ordering to give you time to get here."

"Thank you for waiting. I'll order right now."

"Hurry up. I'm sure you're as hungry as we are."

74 (page 86)

"I've got everything ready for my trip to Argentina."

"When are you leaving, tomorrow?"

"No, next month. But I've got everything ready. The bad thing is that I need some of the things that I packed away. So I keep having to open up my luggage to take something out."

"I think you've packed your luggage too soon. **For the early riser the dawn comes not the sooner.**"

"It's true that **it's not worth it to be overcautious, because it doesn't always yield good results.** But I'm so eager to go on this trip that I couldn't resist the temptation to pack."

75 (page 87)

"What's up, Carlos? I called you yesterday but your line was disconnected. Is anything wrong?"

"I'm the problem, Susana. I'm always behind in my payments. When I get my phone bill, I put it aside and I forget about it."

"Three months ago you had the same problem. You're always procrastinating. **Don't put off for tomorrow what you can do today!**"

"You're right, I shouldn't procrastinate. **The best is to do things as soon as possible.** When I fall behind, I always get in trouble."

"Yes, it's best to do things on time to live in peace."

76 (page 88)

"Luisa, yesterday my team won the first swimming competition of the year. We're going to be this year's champions."

"Not so fast, Marta. **One swallow does not a summer make.**"

"What do you mean by that? Don't you trust our team to win the championship?"

"It's not that I don't trust you, but **one instance doesn't guarantee continued success.** If you really want to win, keep on training."

"I don't know anything about your stories and your swallows. But I can tell you that we are the best. And swallows or not, we are going to win!"

77 (page 89)

[In the graphic design class, the teacher has just finished the lesson and says:]

"Now, take a couple of months to practice with these two computer programs in the lab. That's essential. Remember that **experience is the mother of science.**"

"Professor, we don't want to be scientists, but graphic designers," replies one of the students.

"You think you're funny, right? What I mean is that **if you practice you'll have the experience you need to do a good job.** So, go on to the lab and practice and you will become good graphic designers."

78 (page 90)

"I'm still having problems with Alejandro," says Ana to her mother.

"What's the problem now?"

"He wants me to quit my job and stay home all day."

"What's that about?"

"Oh, Mom! You know he's always been very macho. He says that if I don't quit my job by next month, he'll leave the house and I'll be all alone."

"That's just talk; **it's easier said than done.**"

"You think so?"

"Look, that's just to scare you. **It's easy to say that one is going to do something but it's harder to actually do it.** Stay calm and firm. Talk to him to change that macho attitude. What does your husband think? That we're living in the stone age?"

79 (page 91)

"Fernando, how did you manage to get your mother to loan you her car?"

"You know me, **ask and you shall receive.**"

"Did you talk her into it?"

"Of course, **in order to get something you have to know how to talk to people and convince them.** I explained to her that I really needed to have the car. I promised her I'd fill the gas tank and that I would take care of the washing for the rest of the month. I talked and promised so much, that at the end, she granted my wish."

80 (page 92)

"Vicente, I got another job yesterday. I start this Saturday."

"But, Consuelo, are you dropping out of college?"

"No, of course not. My new job is at a store, just on weekends."

"So, you're quitting your regular office job? Or are you dropping out of your basketball games on Sundays?"

"None of that."

"I think you're crazy. When are you going to get some rest? When are you going to have time to study?"

"Saturday night."

"I'm telling you, you're crazy. **Don't spread yourself too thin.** You won't be able to study well, you won't sleep well, and you won't do your job properly.

"My parents say the same thing. They say that **if you try to do too many things at once, you don't have time to do any of them well.** But I tell them that I can do it all. I'm young and I have a lot of energy."

---

81 (page 93)

"Hi, Olga! How's your son doing in school?"

"He's doing very well. Each year he takes one or two courses. He says he's in no hurry and that way he can study with more care."

"Well, my daughter is about to finish. And I'm sure that she'll find a job before your son does. Tell your son to hurry up, and **not to rest on his laurels.**"

"You're right. I know that **if you don't hurry up, you get behind.** But he's very smart and he studies hard. Your daughter may find a job first, but he will find a better job, in due time. So, leave my son and his laurels alone."

"I only wanted to give you some good advice. Don't you worry about my daughter, because she will certainly find a good job."

---

82 (page 94)

"Oh, Josefa! I'm so upset about Ramoncito!"

"Ramoncito? What happened to him?"

"Nothing yet. The problem is that he now says he wants to be a police officer."

"That's a good thing. What's wrong with that?"

"A police officer? Oh, it's so dangerous! Besides, I wanted my son to be a doctor so I could be proud of him."

"Let Ramoncito choose his own career. **All roads lead to Rome.**"

"Rome? I don't want him to go to Rome!"

"What I mean is that **there are many ways of being successful.** Let him be a police officer if that's what he likes. And you will see how he will succeed and you will feel proud of him, the same as if he were a doctor."

---

83 (page 95)

"Carmen! I'm so glad to see you! What brings you down here?"

"What a surprise, Berta! I'm going to the flower shop to buy some flowers for my mother."

"Is it her birthday?"

"No, no. It's just that yesterday we had a silly argument that left us both upset. I want to make amends with her because she's my best friend."

"You're doing the right thing. **You catch more flies with honey than with vinegar.**"

"That's true. I'm convinced that **you get better results by being kind and cordial toward other people and showing them love and affection, than by mistreating them.** But it's just that my mother is sometimes, let's say... difficult."

"My heart goes out to you. What do you think I'm doing here?"

"You're buying flowers for your mother, too!"

84 (page 96)

"How long do you think it will take us to get to Barcelona, Maricusa?"

"Well, I think that if we go direct, it will be about six hours."

"I was thinking that we could visit my aunt Adela, who lives in Zaragoza. Do you think that we could make a stop there?"

"Of course, Ana. Zaragoza is along the way. We'll be able to rest and eat something there. That way we'll **kill two birds with one stone.**"

"What? What birds are we going to kill?"

"Oh, Ana. What I mean is that we'll be able **to do two things at the same time:** visit your aunt and rest and eat something."

"It's a deal!"

85 (page 97)

"Leonardo, I can't understand how you were able to convince the principal to let us have the party. After all the threats about a student protest, it seemed impossible."

"It wasn't easy, but I succeeded. **Better brain than brawn.**"

"And how brainy were you? Because brawny is one thing you're not, my friend."

"You can make fun of me if you want, but remember who succeeded in our goal. I told him that it would be better to have the students happy, going to many parties, than sad and depressed getting poor grades."

"And that silly argument convinced him?"

"Of course. If we get bad grades and we don't pass, the poor principal will never get rid of us. And that's something he doesn't want to imagine. See how **it's better to solve problems with intelligence instead of violence?**"

86 (page 98)

"Tomorrow Francisca and I are going to paint the house. Do you want to help us?"

"Yes, of course. I also have three or four friends who could help."

"Well, we already have two friends, plus you, Francisca, and myself. All in all, that makes five. The house is not that big. If we bring more people in, **too many cooks could spoil the broth.**"

"If you think that five people is enough..."

"Yes, sometimes, **when too many people try to help, things don't turn out too well.** It's better to have a few organized people than too many disorganized people."

"Anyway, remember that we don't just have arms, but mouths to feed. Will you have food and refreshments for your helpers?"

"Of course we will. We all know what a big eater you are. But remember, if you come it will be to help with the painting. Don't come just to eat and drink."

87 (page 101)

"I'm really upset about the ring I bought for my girlfriend."

"What's wrong? Your girlfriend didn't like it?"

"It's not that. The problem is that I thought it was real gold. It looked very pretty in the sunlight. When I got home, I showed it to my father. He realized that it's not real gold, but gold-painted bronze."

"What a racket! That goes to show you that **all that glitters is not gold.**"

"You're right, **some things are not as valuable as they seem.**"

---

88 (page 102)

"I turn fifty today, but I feel like a thirty-year-old."

"Of course, with the kind of life you lead you'll never get old. You never argue, never raise your voice; don't you have blood running through your veins?"

"Yes, I do and I do care about the world. But **measure is treasure.**"

"You don't say!"

"I do say... **You have to know how to enjoy the finer things in life to stay young.** I stay young because I know how to lead a good life and I surround myself with good things."

---

89 (page 103)

[Two young friends have just come out of the restaurant.]

"Listen, Oscar, why did you want to go out to dinner so early?"

"It's my habit to eat early."

"Well, don't mind me, but you look like an old man eating. You eat very little, like an old man. And old men also have an early dinner. And you don't like to go out dancing at night. Don't you find your life a little dull?"

"You're wrong. **Eat breakfast like a king, lunch like a prince, and dinner like a pauper.**"

"What are you trying to say, that I'm too fat and that I go to bed too late?"

"What I'm telling you is that **in order to stay healthy it's best not to eat too much and to have dinner early** so that you don't go to bed with a full stomach."

"That's the advice of an old man."

---

90 (page 104)

"I'm surprised. Yesterday I saw my philosophy teacher at the gym. She was working out."

"Why does that surprise you?"

"She is very intellectual. I thought people like her use their minds so much that they forget they have a body."

"You're wrong. I think it was actually a philosopher who said: **healthy mind, healthy body.**"

"Well, it seems like she studied that same philosopher, because she knows that **both the mind and the body have to be taken care of.**"

---

91 (page 105)

"My father went to see the doctor yesterday and he was prescribed five medications!"

"Your father doesn't take care of himself."

"He has never eaten well. He has a poor diet, high in fat, and he eats at any

140

time. He has a lot of stomach problems, high blood pressure, high cholesterol, and early diabetes."

"That's why I say that **an apple a day keeps the doctor away.**"

"I agree. **Someone who eats right doesn't need to go to the doctor.**"

---

92 (page 106)

[Mario runs into Julio at a music store. Mario is surprised because Julio never has any money and is always borrowing from friends.]

"Hello, Julio! You seem very happy."

"Yes, I just bought myself a CD of my favorite singer with the last bit of money I had."

"And that makes you happy? It's not good to be left without money. It's more important to keep some money for food than spend it on CDs."

"Oh, Mario! Don't be so serious! Remember that **man does not live by bread alone.** What would life be without music? You like music too, or you wouldn't be here."

"That's true. Besides, **emotional needs are just as important as physical needs.**"

"Since we both agree, are you treating me to lunch?"

---

93 (page 107)

"Did you sell your car, Sara?"

"Yes, it was easy to sell. Someone offered me a little less than what I wanted, but he paid me cash."

"And you thought, **a bird in the hand is worth two in the bush.**"

"Exactly. I could have waited for a better offer, but I don't have the patience. Besides, I didn't know if I would get a better offer."

"Sometimes **it's best to take a sure offer, even if it's not good, than to wait for some better offer that may never come.**"

"At any rate, adding what I got for the old car to my savings gives me enough to buy another car."

---

94 (page 108)

"Things have been going well for Julia and Guillermo at their new business."

"They're very hard working. They always open shop early and they attract many clients. Soon they will expand."

"Like the old saying goes, **the early bird catches the worm.**"

"They are successful because **people who work every day get ahead in life.**"

---

95 (page 109)

"María, why are you so happy?"

"You know very well that I won a bronze medal."

"The one that really counts is the gold medal. A bronze medal is worthless."

"Look, **better something than nothing.** Anyway, do you have any medals?"

"I don't have any medals, not even an aluminum one."

"So, don't make fun of me. I'm happy because **it's better to get an award, even if it's not number one, than not to get any at all.**"

96 (page 110)

"Rafael never has a penny. He never even has enough to pay for a movie."

"How could he, with that expensive car he bought and the luxury apartment he rents?"

"My mother used to say: **stretch your arm no further than your sleeve will reach.**"

"Rafael doesn't act responsibly with his money. **People who live beyond their means can never have any savings.**"

"And what's worse, one day Rafael may find himself in a really serious situation."

"True. He'll have to learn to save money and not waste it."

"I hope he learns soon, or I see him out in the street, without a home or a car!"

97 (page 111)

[Teresa and Felipe have hired a clown for their son's birthday party.]

"Felipe, do you think the clown will want to jump in the pool after the show? It's something that just occurred to me, but we never talked to him about it."

"Let's tell him right away. We can pay him a little more. You know that **money talks.** And the kids would love it."

"Yes, I hope he accepts. **People will do just about anything for money.** Besides, it would be very funny."

98 (page 112)

[After dinner, Cristina takes a third helping of dessert. Her aunt looks at her and says:]

"Cristina, dessert is the end of dinner, not a second meal."

"It's just that I like dessert a lot. You know that."

"Yes, of course I know. But take a look at yourself. You're going to get to be as big as a whale. **Eat to live, not live to eat.** I've always told you."

"Oh, auntie! Let me enjoy my dessert."

"Don't you 'auntie' me. **It's not good to spend all day eating** the way you do. Haven't you looked at yourself in the mirror?"

99 (page 113)

"Good morning, ma'am. I'm the plumber that was referred to you by Mrs. Contreras."

"Good morning, come on in. The job is very simple. You just have to tear this bathroom down and put in a new one. I'll pay you the same as Mrs. Contreras paid you."

"And you expect me to do all this work as **a labor of love?**"

"Not a labor of love. I don't expect you **to work for free.** I said I would pay you the same as Mrs. Contreras."

"Right, but the job I did for Mrs. Contreras was very simple. It was just installing a bathroom sink. Here, we're talking about redoing a whole bathroom. That costs a lot more."

100 (page 114)

"Yolanda, have you heard the latest about Nelson?"

"I'm sure he's got a new story going. What has he come up with now?"

"Now he says that he's going to Madrid to be a bullfighter."

"Are you serious? But didn't he say last week that his agent had found him a supporting role in Hollywood?"

"Well, the story about Madrid is the latest... You know, **it costs nothing to build castles in the air.**"

"It's true that it costs nothing. **It's easy to live from illusions.** Waking up, however, is not the most pleasant thing."

"Here he comes. Let's see what story he has now."

101 (page 115)

[Diego calls Javier on the phone.]

"Javier? How are you? This is Diego."

"I'm fine. How are you?"

"Not so good. I have a big problem. I want to go to this party with Silvia, but my car is broken."

"Don't worry, Diego, I can lend you mine. It's got a full tank of gas and everything. So, you don't have to worry about a thing. I'll bring it over to you right away."

"Listen, you're a really good friend. Look, that money I lent you last week, don't worry about giving it back. It's a **clean slate.**"

"Really?"

"Really. Don't worry about paying back that debt. **We're even now.**"

Index of Proverbs

De tal palo, tal astilla (like father, like son) 22

Del dicho al hecho hay largo trecho (easier said than done) 90

Diente (El) miente, la cana engaña, pero la arruga no ofrece duda (you can't turn back the clock) 28

Dime con quién andas y te diré quién eres (a man is known by the company he keeps) 62

Donde una puerta se cierra, otra se abre (when one door shuts, another opens) 74

E

El que anda con lobos, a aullar se enseña (if you lie down with dogs, you'll get up with fleas) 60

El que dice lo que quiere, oye lo que no quiere (a word once spoken is past recalling) 14

El que no oye consejo no llega a viejo (advice when most needed is least heeded) 29

El que ríe último ríe mejor (he who laughs last, laughs best) 36

El que se fue a Sevilla, perdió la silla (possession is nine-tenths of the law) 9

En boca cerrada no entran moscas (a closed mouth catches no flies) 5

En la unión está la fuerza (in unity there's strength) 52

En martes, ni te cases ni te embarques (never marry or take a trip on Tuesday) 55

Experiencia (La) es la madre de la ciencia (experience is the mother of science) 89

G

Gato (El) escaldado del agua fría huye (once bitten twice shy) 68

Golondrina (Una) no hace el verano (one swallow does not a summer make) 88

H

Hábito (El) no hace al monje (clothes do not make the man) 35

Haz bien y no mires a quién (a good deed is never lost) 53

Haz lo que yo digo y no lo que yo hago (do as I say, not as I do) 15

Hombre prevenido vale por dos (forewarned is forearmed) 33

L

Lo que se aprende en la cuna, hasta la sepultura acompaña (what's learned in the cradle lasts 'til the tomb) 26

Lugar (Un) para cada cosa y cada cosa en su lugar (a place for everything and everything in its place) 11

M

Más moscas se cogen con una gota de miel que con un cuarto de vinagre (you catch more flies with honey than with vinegar) 95

Más sabe el diablo por viejo que por diablo (the devil knows many things because he is old) 21

Más vale malo conocido que bueno por conocer (better the devil you know than the devil you don't) 64

Más vale maña que fuerza (better brain than brawn) 97

Más vale pájaro en mano que ciento volando (a bird in the hand is worth two in the bush) 107

Más vale precaver que tener que lamentar (better safe than sorry) 78

Más vale ser cabeza de ratón que cola de león (better be the head of a dog than the tail of a lion) 18

Más vale tarde que nunca (better late than never) 85

146

Matar dos pájaros de un tiro (to kill
two birds with one stone) 96
Mejor (La) medicina es la buena
comida (an apple a day keeps
the doctor away) 105
Mente sana en cuerpo sano (healthy
mind, healthy body) 104
Mucho hablar y poco decir juntos
suelen ir (empty vessels make
the most noise) 40

N
Niño que no llora no mama (the
squeaky wheel gets the oil) 24
Niños (Los) y los locos dicen las
verdades (out of the mouths of
babes) 27
No dejes para mañana lo que puedas
hacer hoy (don't put off for
tomorrow what you can do
today) 87
No hay mal que por bien no venga
(every cloud has a silver lining)
67
No hay mejor hermano que un buen
vecino al lado (good neighbors
are hard to find) 61
No hay pan sin corteza (cold hands,
warm heart) 4
No hay peor sordo que el que no
quiere oír (there's none so deaf
as those who will not hear) 12
No hay que ahogarse en un vaso de
agua (don't make a mountain
out of a molehill) 69
No hay tonto, por tonto que sea, que
tonto se crea (no fool thinks
he's a fool) 48
No por mucho madrugar amanece
más temprano (for the early
riser the dawn comes not the
sooner) 86
No sólo de pan vive el hombre (man
does not live by bread alone)
106
No todo lo que brilla es oro (all that
glitters is not gold) 101

Nunca es tarde para aprender
(you're never too old to learn)
25

O
Oficio quita vicio (work helps you
stay out of trouble) 16
Ojos que no ven, corazón que no
siente (what the eye doesn't see,
the heart doesn't grieve over)
42

P
Paredes (Las) oyen (walls have
ears) 3
Perro ladrador, poco mordedor
(barking dogs seldom bite) 70
Piensa el ladrón que todos son de su
condición (there is no honor
among thieves) 34
Piso (El) de uno es el techo de otro
(one man's gravy is another
man's poison) 72

Q
Quien buen vino bebe, despacio
envejece (measure is treasure)
102
Quien estudia y no aprende, si no es
asno lo parece (send a donkey
to Paris, and he will return no
wiser than he went) 38
Quien mucho abarca, poco aprieta
(don't spread yourself too thin)
92
Quien nada sabe, de nada duda (he
that knows nothing, doubts
nothing) 37
Quien quisiere vivir sano, coma poco
y cene temprano (eat breakfast
like a king, lunch like a prince,
and dinner like a pauper) 103
Quien siembra vientos recoge tempestades (you reap what you
sow) 77
Quien tiene lengua, a Roma llega
(ask and you shall receive) 91